Retained by the People

Retained by the *People*

The "Silent" Ninth Amendment and the Constitutional Rights Americans Don't Know They Have

DANIEL A. FARBER

Basic Books
A Member of the Perseus Books Group
New York

Designed by Timm Bryson

Library of Congress Cataloging-in-Publication Data

Farber, Daniel A., 1950-
  Retained by the people : the "silent" Ninth Amendment and the constitutional rights
Americans don't know they have / Daniel Farber.
     p. cm.
  Includes bibliographical references and index.
  ISBN-13: 978-0-465-02298-4 (hardcover : alk. paper)
  ISBN-10: 0-465-02298-7 (hardcover : alk. paper) 1. United States. Constitution. 9th
Amendment. 2. Civil rights--United States. 3. Constitutional law--United States. I. Title.

KF45589th .F37 2007
342.7308'5--dc22
                                          2007005520

10 9 8 7 6 5 4 3 2 1

To Mike, Lisa, and Jackie
"Quid nunc?"

Contents

PART III

APPLYING THE NINTH AMENDMENT

PART IV

BROADER IMPLICATIONS

Preface

The enumeration in the Constitution, of certain
rights, shall not be construed to deny or disparage others retained by the people.

—THE NINTH AMENDMENT

Everyone knows about the First Amendment right of free speech
and the Fifth Amendment right to avoid self-incrimination. Even
the once-forgotten Second Amendment, with its "right to bear
arms," has reemerged in public debate. But few people know about
the Ninth Amendment, which reaffirms in broad terms rights "retained by the people." Indeed, the Ninth flies so far under the radar
that it has rarely been mentioned even by the Supreme Court.

What a pity. Even more, what a terrible oversight: the Ninth
Amendment bears directly on such modern-day constitutional issues as abortion, the right to die, and gay rights.

The Ninth Amendment is key to understanding how the Founding Fathers thought about the liberties they expected Americans to
enjoy under the Constitution. They did not believe that they were
creating these liberties in the Bill of Rights. Instead, they were
merely *acknowledging* some of the rights that no government could
properly deny. The history of the Constitution reveals the purpose
of the Ninth and the Founders' intent: to protect what constitutional lawyers call unenumerated rights—those rights the Founders

assumed and felt no need to specify in the Bill of Rights. Unenumerated rights include, for example, the right to privacy. In the America
of today, unenumerated rights account for freedoms like a woman's
right to abortion.

By delving into the history and the ideas that shaped the values of
the Founding Fathers, I will attempt to clarify the Ninth and thrust
it into the pivotal role it deserves in resolving our thorny constitutional debates. The truth is that anyone interested in the political
and legal issues of the day can and should look to the Ninth Amendment for guidance.

The Ninth Amendment is paired with an almost equally forgotten provision, the Privileges or Immunities Clause (P or I Clause) of
the Fourteenth Amendment, which draws from the same intellectual roots. The Ninth Amendment is like the rest of the original Bill
of Rights: it speaks only to limits on federal power rather than to
the powers of state governments. Limitations on state governments
came along later, with the post–Civil War Fourteenth Amendment.
Thus, the Ninth Amendment addresses the federal government; the
Fourteenth addresses the states.

The human rights vision that survived the Civil War and was
confirmed by the Fourteenth Amendment consciously comple-
ments that of the Founders. Confronting what these provisions
really mean has the potential to reshape the way we think about
the Constitution.

In particular, a look at this history helps us address the very controversial question of Supreme Court reliance on foreign law. The
Framers thought that fundamental rights were embedded in what
they called "the law of nations," and we should follow their lead in
seeking inspiration abroad. However, their openness to foreign law
is not universally shared today. When Justice Kennedy referred to
foreign law in two judicial opinions on the issues of homosexuality
and the death penalty, he was subject to an onslaught of criticism

from legal commentators. Many of those same commentators question whether the United States is bound by international human rights laws, such as the Geneva Convention's prohibitions on mistreatment of prisoners.

My goal in this book is not to provide an encyclopedic view of how the Founding Fathers or their Civil War successors thought about rights. That would take a book two or three times as long as this one. Such a tome would allow me to indulge my scholarly inclinations. It would give full scope to probe ambiguities and inconsistencies in the historical record and to tease out the complex interplay between political forces and conceptual developments. But this is not the place for such a detailed historical exploration. Instead, I have emphasized the key developments and tried to provide a coherent narrative of those developments, which generally follows the views of leading current historians such as Jack Rakove and Gordon Wood.

This book was a long time in the making. It is the culmination of research that I started at the beginning of my career with John Muench, who later left teaching to become a stellar appellate lawyer. It also builds on my work on constitutional history with my former colleague and frequent coauthor, Suzanna Sherry. I am particularly in debt to her work on the intellectual context of the Framing era and on judicial enforcement of unwritten constitutional rights. Readers who wish to see the relevant portions of the historical documents I discuss can find most of them in a book we wrote together, *A History of the American Constitution*.[1] The endnotes in the current volume contain only references to a few secondary sources and some hard-to-locate primary sources. Sources such as the Federalist Papers are not footnoted since they are easy to locate in most libraries.

It is customary to end prefaces such as this with thanks to family for their support during the writing process. Such thanks are unusually appropriate in this case. During the time I was writing this book, I also felt an obligation to work on some of the issues arising from Hurricane Katrina, which combined with this writing took up almost all of my time for the past year. Not only were they remarkably tolerant, but my wife, Dianne, and my daughter, Sonia, took time to help greatly with the final edit. Hopefully, it was all in a good cause.

Dan Farber

A Reference Chart of Constitutional Provisions

If you're not a lawyer, you may have trouble keeping track of the various constitutional provisions discussed in this book. This chart may help. The entries are roughly in order of how often the provision is mentioned in the book.

CONSTITUTIONAL GUARANTEE	MEANING	LOCATION IN THE CONSTITUTION
"Rights retained by the people"	Protection of fundamental rights from violations by the federal government	Ninth Amendment
"P or I" Clause	Protects fundamental rights ("privileges or immunities") from state government	Fourteenth Amendment (post–Civil War)
Equal Protection Clause	Prohibits discrimination by states	Fourteenth Amendment
Due Process Clause	Requires government to provide due process. The core meaning of due process is a "fair hearing," but the idea has been extended to include protection for fundamental rights	Found in two places: the Fifth Amendment (as a limit on the federal government) and the Fourteenth Amendment (as a limit on the states)
Tenth Amendment	Protects powers reserved to state governments	Tenth Amendment (surprise!)

Constitutional Guarantee	Meaning	Location in the Constitution
Bill of Rights	First eight amendments protect specific rights like free speech from federal government, followed by ninth and tenth Amendments	Amendments One through Ten (proposed and ratified a few years after the original Constitution was adopted)
Thirteenth Amendment	Abolished slavery	Thirteenth Amendment (post–Civil War)
Fifteenth Amendment	Gave blacks the right to vote	Fifteenth Amendment (post–Civil War)
Necessary and Proper Clause	Gives Congress the power to make all laws necessary and proper to carry out specific powers such as regulation of interstate commerce	Article I of the 1789 Constitution

Another provision I will sometimes refer to is the P and I Clause, a provision in Article IV that prohibits any state from discriminating against citizens of other states. This has almost the same language as the P *or* I Clause in the Fourteenth Amendment but has been interpreted narrowly in recent years. It is relevant to our discussion only because the Framers of the Fourteenth Amendment used it as a model.

I

Who's Afraid of the Ninth Amendment?

The enumeration in the Constitution, of
certain rights, shall not be construed to deny
or disparage others retained by the people

The Ninth Amendment is a constitutional orphan, forgotten by most and reviled by some—especially on the conservative end of the spectrum. One of the only exceptions is Justice Arthur Goldberg's concurring opinion in the famous *Griswold* case, which upheld the right of married couples to use birth control.[1] Yes, there was a time, only four decades ago, when some states made this a crime. Some jurists still do not see any constitutional problem with such legislation; it is no coincidence that they seek to keep the Ninth Amendment safely neutered.

In the contraception case Justice Goldberg recounted some of the history of the Ninth Amendment. He reminded his fellow judges that "since 1791 it has been a basic part of the Constitution which we are sworn to uphold." As he demonstrated, the language and history of the Ninth Amendment show that the Framers of the Constitution believed in additional fundamental rights, protected from governmental violation, alongside those listed in the Bill of

Rights. But Goldberg's remarks were a rare departure from the usual pattern of judicial deafness toward the Amendment, and they were rapidly forgotten.

While political parties clash over the morality underlying these rights, lawyers and judges debate their legality. "Unenumerated rights," the lawyer's term for these unlisted fundamental rights, is the battlefield on which these struggles play out. Most Americans are unfamiliar with this term, yet it determines how free we are to make the decisions that shape our private lives. And it is the great, and wholly American, ideal that gives the Ninth Amendment its meaning.

The Ninth Amendment does not stand alone in the Constitution. A similar provision in the Fourteenth Amendment guarantees each of us the "privileges or immunities of citizens of the United States." The drafters of this provision, like the original Founding Fathers, believed in the existence of natural rights. Unlike the Ninth Amendment, which was adopted with an eye toward abuses by the federal government, the Fourteenth Amendment protects rights against violation by state governments.

So why haven't the Ninth and its Fourteenth Amendment counterpart had more impact on the war of constitutional interpretations that has plagued Congress and the courts for the last twenty years? Because their meaning is implied, linked as they are to history and an understanding of what the Framers believed. Thus their purpose seems easy to dispute and distort.

Both provisions also came at the peak of an interest in individual rights but were soon relegated to obscurity when states' rights emerged as the more pressing concern. Through a series of historical accidents, the Supreme Court later ended up attaching fundamental rights to another—and less appropriate—part of the Constitution, the Due Process Clause of the Fourteenth Amendment. The result has been conceptual confusion and vulnerability to conservative critiques.

The Conservative Flight from the Ninth Amendment

Liberals (for lack of a better term) have as yet to directly embrace the Ninth. They argue the case for rights on the basis of clauses like Due Process or give up on fundamental rights in favor of arguments based on discrimination law. I believe that's because they find the Ninth too elusive. Buried as it is in eighteenth-century ideas, in debates among the Founders as they wrote the Constitution, and in James Madison's oratory before Congress, the Ninth seems shadowy, a battle that cannot be won.

For historical reasons, the Supreme Court has mostly protected fundamental rights under the guise of the Due Process Clause rather than the Ninth Amendment. For many liberals it has not seemed to matter much that this was the wrong clause, with the wrong language and the wrong historical background. But it does matter. Today, text and history have become crucial to constitutional argument. We should not let the opponents of personal freedom lay claim to these crucial forms of support. The Constitution and the Framers' vision are potent allies of anyone arguing for liberty. And in protecting rights already granted by law, the Supreme Court has begun to take this vision into account.

It is conservatives who should fear and deny the Ninth—and many do, especially the so-called movement conservatives who make up the "base." Those who seek to legislate the private decisions of millions of Americans will strenuously object to this book, and for good reason. The Ninth challenges both what they believe about the Constitution and what they publicly offer as their rationale for imposing their morality on others. To most conservatives, the Bill of Rights is complete: the Framers meant nothing other than what it explicitly says. For all their talk about fidelity to the Constitution, however, they prefer to ignore inconvenient parts of it.

Since many conservatives do not want to hear its message, they pretend that the Ninth does not exist. They claim that, with its murky language, it is a meaningless fragment, not at all amenable to intelligible interpretation. Robert Bork compared the Ninth to an "ink blot" during his confirmation hearings. He said, "I do not think the court can make up what might be under the ink blot if you cannot read it." In other words, unenumerated rights simply do not exist.

Other conservatives argue that the Amendment was really intended to protect states' rights, either by requiring strict construction of federal powers or by preventing the federal government from overriding state laws and constitutional provisions. Apart from a few libertarians, who are well out of the mainstream of political influence within the conservative movement, conservatives have no use for the Ninth Amendment.

Both the Bork view and the states' rights argument are strained and desperate efforts to avoid the plain meaning of the Amendment. All we have to do is look fully at what it says. It speaks of rights "retained by the people," not rights "retained by the states." It openly tells us that by listing some rights, the Constitution does not thereby "deny or disparage others retained by the people."

The Framers picked their words carefully and understood just what they were doing. They meant the Bill of Rights to be *illustrative*, not complete: the Ninth Amendment adds a crucial "etc." to the Bill. This "etc." represents the liberties the Framers viewed as fundamental—rights that were part of their political and ethical vision, what they had fought a revolution to honor. For them, as men of their time, these rights were based in "natural law" and the "law of nations." These two terms had significant meaning for the Framers and were expansively defined.

Some conservatives acknowledge that the Ninth Amendment, like the Declaration of Independence, refers to innate human rights.

But they contend that these unenumerated rights lack any *legal* weight and were merely entrusted to the political process. This theory conveniently allows these conservatives to pretend belief in innate rights without ever having to do anything about them.

Justice Scalia put forward this theory in a case involving parental rights that I will discuss in detail later in this book. He conceded that a right of parents to bring up their children is among the inalienable rights of the Declaration of Independence. It was also, he said, among the right retained by the people under the Ninth Amendment. So far, so good. But according to Justice Scalia these rights are paper tigers, without any legal effect. For Scalia, the Ninth Amendment's refusal "to 'deny or disparage' other rights is far removed from affirming any one of them." The Ninth is also, he said, "even further removed" from authorizing judges to identify and enforce those rights. In other words, it is fine to make use of the Ninth in political debate. Yet, Justice Scalia said, he lacked any power as a judge to strike down these laws when in his opinion they infringe upon a valid unenumerated right.

The specific case before him involved the right of parents to bring up their children; according to Justice Scalia, this right has no legal standing. This is a peculiar position—if you read Justice Scalia's opinion carefully, he seems to be saying that the right of parents to raise their own offspring *is* an unenumerated right *and* that it is covered as such by the Ninth Amendment. The trouble is that for Scalia, the Ninth Amendment speaks to him when he is a citizen but not when he puts on his black robe and climbs on the bench. When you think about it, Scalia's view is even less defensible than Judge Bork's. Bork said that he could not enforce the Ninth Amendment because he has no way of figuring out what it means; Scalia seems to say that he does know what it means, but he won't enforce it anyway.

For the most part, in this book I will put forward the best interpretation of history without delving into the debate that swirls around some of these issues. However, readers who want a more detailed re-buttal of some alternative explanations should turn to the Appendix on "Misunderstanding the Framers" at the end of the book.

FUNDAMENTAL RIGHTS AND THE FOUNDING FATHERS

Given what we know about the legal thinking at the time the Consti-tution was written, the Ninth Amendment cannot be dismissed as a mere moral admonition, devoid of legal import. Fundamental rights had their roots in natural law and the law of nations, and these were not merely collections of pious wishes to embroider political rheto-ric. In the Framers' view, these rights had very real legal application.

The Framers took seriously the idea that government has no le-gitimate authority to violate human rights, regardless of what spe-cific laws might say. We can never understand the Ninth Amendment until we grasp that basic premise of the Founding Fa-thers: human rights come first, and legal regimes come second.

This was the axiom proclaimed in the Declaration of Indepen-dence: "all men are endowed by their Creator with certain inalienable rights." The Declaration embodied the perspective of natural law: that individual rights are not simply privileges granted in legal docu-ments, but instead they are the birthright of all humans everywhere.

The idea of natural law had broad intellectual support in the eighteenth century. Of the natural law writers who were familiar to the Framers, the philosopher John Locke is clearly the best known today. His theory of the state of nature and the social compact pro-vided a philosophical foundation for natural rights.

Locke's theory is based on the idea of the state of nature, in which individuals are free from all government. In this state of na-ture, individuals are subject to certain natural duties and possess certain natural rights. Among these natural rights are the right to continued life and the right to whatever property is created by one's own labor. All individuals are equal in the sense of having an equal right to this natural freedom. Unfortunately, in the state of nature, although all have equal rights, they are also equally vulnerable to the invasion of their rights by others. The solution is to band together to protect their rights.

In Locke's view government comes into existence when people create a central authority by means of a social contract. This authority has only the power it is granted through this delegation or compact, that is, the power to protect individuals in their natural rights. "The law of nature stands as an eternal rule to all men, legislators as well as others."[2]

Although they have been largely forgotten today, three other writers of the school of natural law were highly influential in eighteenth- and early nineteenth-century America. These were Samuel Pufendorf, Emmerich de Vattel, and Jean Jacques Burlamaqui. As his major modern commentator says, "Samuel Pufendorf is known to American students—when he is known at all—as an obscure German with a funny name who followed Grotius in the early development of international law."[3] Nevertheless, he was a highly influential thinker.

Pufendorf's natural law system stressed the social nature of human beings and their duty to protect each other's welfare. Like Locke, he also stressed human equality and the compact theory of government. Pufendorf was no obscure figure at the time: sixteen editions of his most famous work on natural law were published in England in the decades before the American Revolution.

Burlamaqui's theory shared the same theological foundation underlying Locke's work. In his view, since God gave humans life and the desire for happiness, God must have wanted them to pursue these goals, thereby imposing on other people the duty not to interfere with these rights. Like Pufendorf and Locke, Burlamaqui adopted a compact theory of government under which government acts in excess of the granted power were invalid.

Vattel's work mainly involved international law but contained some important observations on natural law. He postulated that society is obliged to preserve its members and cannot override their natural right to self-defense. If the sovereign violates fundamental rights, the nation as a whole can withdraw its obedience. Vattel's extensive writings on international law have been deeply influential in terms of U.S. law—for example, he has been cited more than 150 times by the United States Supreme Court, including as recently as 2004.

For the Framers, unlike Justice Scalia, natural law was not a legally irrelevant moral theory. And natural law ideas were not simply a passing expression of revolutionary fervor. Natural law continued to play an important role in American law well into the nineteenth century. In particular, natural law ideas influenced the drafters of the Fourteenth Amendment at the end of the Civil War.

One of the best-known early instances of reliance on natural law was the 1798 Calder opinion by Justice Samuel Chase. In that opinion, written soon after the Constitution went into effect, he declared that state governments were limited by "certain vital principles in our free Republican governments, which will determine and overrule an apparent and flagrant abuse of legislative power." Less well-known are opinions by Chief Justice John Marshall taking the same position. Like the Framers, Marshall understood that government authority is subject to inherent limits. A host of state law decisions articulated the same view. In short, natural law was not a dead letter for the Founding Fathers; it was hard, enforceable *law*.

I believe that when the Supreme Court protects an unenumerated right like privacy, it is simply doing what the Framers directed. And in denying the existence of those kinds of rights, conservatives are doing precisely what the Framers feared: denying or disparaging the rights retained by the people.

In addition, when conservatives spurn the Ninth, they miss the deep irony of their standard of constitutional interpretation. They argue that laws must be judged strictly according to the original intent of the Founders (a theory called "originalism") and that the text of the Constitution must be applied as written. Well, in this dispute, the Constitution speaks very plainly. Is the list of specific rights protected by the Constitution complete? The Ninth answers, "Of course not," clearly and succinctly. All of us, conservative or liberal, would do well to heed it.

The Ninth Amendment and the Debate over Fundamental Rights

Standing alone, the Ninth Amendment does not make any specific law unconstitutional. It is an explanation, not a command—like the FAQs found on many Web sites. In this case, the Frequently Asked Question is: "The Bill of Rights provides a list of specific rights that are protected from invasion by the federal government. Does this mean that the federal government can violate other rights if they aren't on the list?" The Ninth answers, "No. The Bill of Rights is not complete. Other rights exist, and the federal government must respect them." Indeed, as a supporter of the Constitution pointed out at the Pennsylvania ratification convention, "Our rights are not yet all known," so an enumeration was impossible.[4] While it is true that history often fails to provide clear proof of what the Framers believed, there are exceptions. The Ninth Amendment is one of them.

How is all this playing out on our most vital constitutional front, the Supreme Court, today? The Court is sharply divided over whether the Constitution provides broad protection for human rights and just what those rights are. On one side have been those Justices who believe that the Constitution does give such broad protection—not just to those freedoms explicitly listed in the Bill of Rights but to other fundamental aspects of liberty. In honoring not merely the Framers' text but the intent behind it, these Justices have supported, for example, the right to abortion, the right of gays to have sexual relationships, and the right to die. More generally, these Justices have proclaimed: "At the heart of liberty is the right to define one's own concept of existence, of meaning, of the universe, and of the mystery of human life."[5]

These Justices also honor the Framers' intent by looking beyond our national borders to seek the parameters of liberty. For example, in striking down a Texas law against homosexual conduct, the Court found it significant that the right to engage in homosexual relationships has "been accepted as an integral part of human freedom in many other countries." On today's bench, Justice Stevens has been a leading advocate of this view. However, its most influential voice is that of the more conservative Justice, Anthony Kennedy. Kennedy, a Reagan appointee, has become the bête noire of movement conservatives because he has so firmly defended basic rights and linked those rights to international law.

The opposing side is led by Justice Antonin Scalia, another Reagan appointee. As a former law professor at the University of Chicago and the University of Virginia, and now as a judge, Scalia has spent years working out an elaborate constitutional theory of originalism. He has consistently dissented from the entire line of human rights cases, arguing that abortion, gay rights, and end-of-life decisions should all be left entirely to the political process. This is a view that has powerful backing outside the Supreme Court. President Bush has renewed calls for strict construction of the Constitution (by which he means strict limits on individual rights, but apparently not strict construction of the powers of the Presidency!).

More extremist views, replete with threats of impeachment or other unprecedented actions to rein in judges, can be found in Congress and among the Right's cultural leadership. Nothing is more anathema to these critics than the Court's reliance on foreign judicial precedents as a source of guidance in interpreting the Constitution. Justice Scalia warned of the Court's "dangerous" references to foreign law, adding that "this Court . . . should not impose foreign moods, fads, or fashions on Americans." He and his fellow critics see no connection between broader conceptions of human rights and constitutional law. They refuse to look seriously at what the Framers believed, how they saw the world.

Some conservatives also seemingly misunderstand the very idea of constitutional rights. Are basic rights like free speech or privacy created by the U.S. Constitution? For many conservatives, these rights are merely the historical product of particular language adopted a century or two in the past; they have no broader roots or implications. If so, Justice Kennedy was surely wrong in the Texas sodomy case when he examined a much broader range of sources, including how states interpret their own constitutions, the actions taken by state legislatures to decriminalize sodomy, and the rulings of international tribunals. These sources are relevant only if we ask a broader question: "Are there good grounds for considering this to be a basic human right?" If that is the question, then actions by state legislatures, state judges, and international human rights tribunals are all persuasive authorities. The Founders certainly understood the law of nations and basic liberty in this way.

Rephrasing the question in these terms also rebuts another powerful argument against providing constitutional protection for human rights. Justice Scalia and others have argued that going beyond the specifics of the Bill of Rights would give the Supreme Court unlimited discretion to decide what parts of liberty are fundamental. This was the real concern that led Judge Bork to call the

Ninth Amendment an inkblot: the fear that if we paid any attention to the Ninth Amendment at all, we would be mesmerized into giving the federal judiciary a blank check. This is much less problematic if the courts are guided by a broader community of opinion, including our own state decision makers as well as international authorities.

To see what is at stake, consider a 1927 Supreme Court case that upheld compulsory sterilization. The Virginia statute involved in the case established a procedure for sterilizing people with mental retardation who lived in state institutions, based on the idea that mental disability was inherited. The statute was challenged by a woman who was about to be sterilized. As later historical research revealed, she actually did not have a mental disability at all; she simply had been sent to an institution by her foster parents because she had become pregnant. In any event, the Supreme Court could not see any problem with the Virginia statute: "It is better for all the world, if instead of waiting to execute degenerate offspring for crime, or to let them starve for their imbecility, society can prevent those who are manifestly unfit from continuing their kind. . . . Three generations of imbeciles are enough." By 1935, over twenty thousand forced sterilizations had been performed in the United States as a result of this decision.

If mainstream conservatives like Bork and Scalia are right, there is no constitutional barrier to these laws, because the Framers failed to predict this abuse and explicitly ban it. This is exactly the kind of reasoning that the Ninth Amendment was designed to guard against. A better understanding of the Ninth Amendment can do a great deal to clarify the current debate over fundamental rights, laying a firm foundation for the views of Justice Kennedy and other leading judges. Correspondingly, a true understanding of the Ninth Amendment is deadly to Justice Scalia's position.

Libertarians, who dislike government regulation of all kinds, agree with part of my argument, and I have found much of their historical research useful. They, too, would find the Amendment to be a source of real legal guidance. But they swing too far in the opposite direction from conservatives like Scalia. While Scalia wants the Ninth Amendment to protect nothing, the libertarians want it to protect virtually everything. They see in it the basis of a revolutionary return to the small government ideas of the early nineteenth century. But this is a gross overreading of the Amendment. It was meant to protect fundamental human rights, not just the right to do whatever you want whenever you want.

THE ROAD AHEAD

In the remainder of this book, I will try to make good on these bold claims. The first half of the book is historical: I will show how the Ninth Amendment grew out of the Framers' worldview about law and rights, and I will rebut conservative claims that it had no genuine content. I will also show how similar ideas bore fruit after the Civil War in another forgotten part of the Constitution, the Privileges or Immunities Clause of the Fourteenth Amendment.

This review of history should be especially important for originalists. Originalists claim to base their constitutional views on the historical intent of the Framers. Most non-originalists also agree that the views of the Framers are important, even if we do not think they provide the final answer to all questions. The main difference is that non-originalists believe that history is better as a source of general principles than specific directives. Originalists tend to believe that history provides very specific guidance about modern disputes. Unfortunately, the clear and detailed answers they purport to find often seem to be based on a selective or superficial understanding of the historical record.

The second half of the book shows how the Ninth Amendment can shed light on current constitutional issues. I will explain the

Supreme Court's current approach to fundamental rights cases and demonstrate how the Ninth Amendment could be used in a sensible way, not just as an open-ended invitation for judges to select their own preferred social values for constitutional protection. I will then apply these lessons to specific disputes such as gay rights, the right to die, and the right to an education. To anticipate, here are some of the things I believe are among the unenumerated rights protected by the Constitution under the Ninth Amendment, backed up by the Fourteenth:

- The right to engage in private sexual acts between consenting adults. The Supreme Court was completely correct to strike down state sodomy laws.
- The right of reproductive autonomy, including the use of contraceptives and access to abortion as well as freedom from forced sterilization. Abortion is not an absolute right. The state can regulate to protect potential life, particularly later in pregnancy, so long as the burden placed on the pregnant woman is not too severe.
- The right to an adequate basic education. The Supreme Court has explicitly rejected this as a fundamental constitutional right, but many state courts have interpreted their state constitutions to protect this right. The Supreme Court would do well to follow their lead.
- The right to travel within the United States and to enter and leave the country freely (subject to clearly demonstrated national security needs).
- The right to government protection from private violence: when the government knows of the violence and has the resources to deal with the problem, it cannot simply sit on its hands. The Supreme Court has ruled that the state has every right to sit by while a

small boy is beaten into a permanent coma by his father, even though the state knows all about what is going on. I would overturn that decision.
- The right to refuse unwanted medical treatment, including the right of terminally ill patients to reject life
  support.

But not everything is protected as a fundamental right. Here are
some things that are not:

- The right of a terminally ill patient to prescribed medication with which to commit suicide.
- The right of businesses to be free from government regulation of their contracts with employees and customers.
- The right of individuals to use their property however
  they want, without regard to the public interest.

This book is not a call for a constitutional revolution. In terms of
specific issues, much of the ground has already been traveled by the
Supreme Court, although under the guise of other constitutional
provisions. But the Supreme Court's approach to fundamental
rights has been very much on the defensive, under attack from jurists like Justice Scalia and social conservatives in Congress and the
White House.

In this book, I am seeking to revive our understanding of the
American tradition of reverence for fundamental rights. That tradition provides a firm foundation for the Court's decisions. There is
no reason to apologize for what the Court has done or for timidly
refusing to take further steps when they are called for. In short, advocates of fundamental rights should stop being defensive and
should make it clear that they, rather than their opponents, best represent the American constitutional tradition.

Some Guidelines for the Reader

Several observations are in order before we turn to the history of the Ninth Amendment. The first is about terminology.

Strictly speaking, the Ninth Amendment does not create any rights; it simply upholds the vitality of existing rights. The Fourteenth Amendment then provides a federal guarantee against violations of those rights by state government. So technically, the rights involved should be referred to as "those rights preserved by the Ninth Amendment in terms of federal power and protected from state violation by the Fourteenth Amendment." But this would be unbearably clumsy. So I will frequently refer to those rights simply as "Ninth Amendment rights" or "fundamental rights." In accordance with historical terminology, I also sometimes refer to them as "natural rights" or "human rights." By doing so I am not making any large philosophical claims about how rights originate. Whether the source is divine sanction, the social contract, the inherent nature of human dignity, or evolving social values, the key point is that these rights are basic to our understanding of individual freedom in modern society.

I also want to be clear that my argument for resurrecting the Ninth Amendment is emphatically not a plea for judicial activism. The biggest concern about judicial enforcement of unenumerated rights is that they can be abused by judges who simply want to pursue their own political agenda. Whether we are talking about enumerated rights like the First Amendment or the unenumerated rights of the Ninth, judicial impartiality, common sense, and humility are invaluable. Although conservatives fear that judicial activism will be fueled if U.S. courts look to foreign precedent, this may be backwards: the absence of strong international support for recognizing a right may caution our courts against being too adventuresome.

In any event, if we are concerned about judicial activism, the threat is just as much from overzealous conservatives as from liberals. Justices who lack self-restraint and confuse their personal political views with the Constitution are equally dangerous, with or without the Ninth Amendment. The solution to judicial activism is to select good judges, not to distort history in the hope of limiting the arena for judicial misadventures.

Judicial restraint is not incompatible with recognizing unenumerated rights. Justice John Harlan, a dissenter from many of the Warren Court's most "activist" decisions, was also the strongest advocate for protecting unenumerated rights. But he was cast from a different mold from that of many of today's conservative legal thinkers. After examining the deep historical foundations for protecting fundamental rights, I will show how judges can be guided by the constitutional text, evolving traditions, and precedents both American and international.

PART ONE

Unwritten Rights and the Constitution

2

Natural Rights and the Framers

To understand the Ninth Amendment, we need to first understand how the Founding Fathers thought about rights. Some of their views would seem familiar to us, such as their insistence that rights are not merely a gift from generous lawmakers. But other parts of their intellectual framework, such as their conception of what they called "the law of nations," diverge strikingly from modern notions.

One thing we have inherited from the Framers is a belief in inalienable rights. We also expect at least some of these rights to be protected by law, not just by political sentiment. As historian Bernard Bailyn recently remarked, we are heirs to their insight "that there is a sense, mysterious as it may be, in which human rights can be seen to exist independent of privileges, gifts, and donations of the powerful, and that these rights can somehow be defined and protected by the force of law."[1] Bailyn, who has profoundly influenced current historians' understanding of early American thought, has the support of volumes of evidence. The historical record shows that the idea of natural rights was pervasive during the Founding era. Another leading historian of the period, Jack Rakove, has made the point especially clearly: the "language of rights came naturally to the colonists; it was, they thought, their native tongue."[2]

Most famously, the Declaration of Independence embodies the idea of natural rights—legal rights that do not derive their validity from any specific enactment but from fundamental moral principles: "we hold these truths to be self-evident, that all men are created equal and endowed by their creator with certain unalienable rights, among them life, liberty and the pursuit of happiness." To us, the Declaration may seem not only literally but also figuratively a bit of "Fourth of July" rhetoric. But for the Framers, this language had a solid intellectual foundation, which we ignore at our peril in seeking to understand them.

Another famous example—famous among historians, anyway—is James Otis's argument against the right of Parliament to authorize writs of assistance (basically blank checks to officials to search wherever they wanted). He argued that courts were obligated to void laws that violate fundamental rights: "As to Acts of Parliament, an Act against the Constitution is void: an Act against natural Equity is void. . . . Courts must pass such Acts into disuse." (An act that was "against the Constitution" was contrary to the core guarantees of English law, such as Magna Charta, or violated the basic structure of government.) Similarly, in protesting the Stamp Act, the American colonists turned to the courts for support, contending that the Act was unconstitutional and therefore void.

Today, people often think of rights as being created by laws. For example, we might say that the First Amendment creates the constitutional right to free speech. But the Framers didn't think this way—as the Declaration puts it, these rights are endowed by God, not by a human enactment. Because the rights are inalienable, control over them cannot be transferred from the individuals themselves to the government. Beyond any specific enactments of legislators, certain rights have their own existence and must be respected by everyone alike.

The Framers found intellectual support for this concept in the work of great lawyers such as Sir Edward Coke as well as philosophers like Locke. It was Coke who said that "when an Act of Parliament is against a common right and reason, or repugnant, or impossible to be performed, the common law will controul it, and adjudge such Act to be void."[3] Thus, according to Coke, legislation was subject to overriding mandates rather than merely the political whim of the majority.

In the present era, the most vibrant reflection of this idea is in the international law of human rights. We think that all governments are required to respect certain key human rights, whether or not their own national constitutions or legislation recognize those rights. Where we may differ from the Framers is how we conceptualize this mandate: as a purely moral requirement or as also a legal imperative. We tend to think of these rights as moral imperatives, but not necessarily as having any direct legal force until they are translated into specific laws or treaties. The Framers, on the other hand, believed that this framework of human rights was very much relevant to the operation of the legal system.

The idea of natural rights fits easily within the system of the common law. The common law draws on many sources, including judicial precedents, social values, applicable (or sometimes merely analogous) legislation, writings by scholars, and decisions on similar issues by courts in other jurisdictions. To the extent that each of these factors finds its way into the court's written opinion, lawyers have to treat them all as part of "the law."

Natural law was an important part of English common law. The eminent legal historian R. H. Helmholz recently undertook a thorough survey of the impact of natural law on the English common law.[4] He has compiled a list of more than sixty leading English legal writers who endorsed natural law as part of the common law before the American Revolution. The list included many of the great names of English legal history such as Lord Coke, Lord Mansfield, and Matthew Hale—not to mention one bona fide saint (Thomas More).

These thinkers, Helmholz concluded, saw natural law as a legitimate source of English law, not an exotic foreign import. He also observed that the idea of natural law surfaced in some of the common law's most famous cases. For instance, a case from 1468 referred to the law of nature as "the ground of all laws" and described it as the basis for decision when precedents were lacking. English lawyers did not draw any sharp distinction between the common law and natural law, for they assumed that reason and natural law "stood behind and supported the English common law."[5] Similarly, as Jack Rakove explains, colonists did not "regard English rights as a weak alternative to the great natural rights of mankind; English rights were the legal application of natural rights."[6]

OUR COSMOPOLITAN FRAMERS: U.S. LAW AND THE "LAW OF NATIONS"

As their intimate knowledge of writers like Locke, Vattel, and Burlamqui indicated, the Framers had a global intellectual vision. Many of today's conservatives are aghast that the Supreme Court looks beyond our own borders. The Founding Fathers and their successors were far more cosmopolitan.

A few conservative scholars have acknowledged as much. For example, Steven Calabresi, one of the cofounders of the archconservative Federalist Society, has conceded that the "Supreme Court's practice of citing and relying on foreign law goes back two centuries and is far more deeply rooted in the Court's caselaw than is the fabled and much discussed right to privacy or even the New Deal. If precedent and caselaw count for anything in constitutional law, then the legitimacy of Supreme Court citation of foreign laws is a long settled question."

Certainly, the Framers had no qualms about looking to foreign and international law. They frequently took guidance from what they called "the law of nations." The law of nations has no exact counterpart today; it was a blend of legal fields we would now consider quite distinct, including international law and commercial law.

According to one influential American judge and legal commentator, the law of nations derived from "principles of right reason, the same views of the nature and constitution of man, and the same sanction of Divine revelation, as those from which the science of morality is deduced."[7] Key elements of the law of nations were the "general principles of right and justice, equally suitable to the government of individuals in a state of natural equality, and to the relations and conduct of nations."[8]

The idea of an unwritten international law was very much in tune with the thinking of the legal community in the nineteenth century. Today, we think of the common law as being specific to each individual state or country. But until the twentieth century, the common law was considered to be a separate entity, shared by *all* common law courts, rather than a mere aspect of a specific state's law. In the early nineteenth-century case of *Swift v. Tyson*,[9] the Supreme Court held that federal courts would apply the "general common law" rather than the rulings of any particular state court in resolving disputes. In setting down this rule, the Court drew a phrase from Roman law meant to emphasize the universality of these legal principles. These rules, it was said, are "not just the law of Rome or Athens or any one place, but the law of all people at all times." Today, the Court has repudiated the view of the common law as a repository of universal principles. But to early Americans, this view came very naturally.

The Constitution itself acknowledges the law of nations. Article I of the Constitution empowers Congress to define and punish "Offences against the Law of Nations." Accordingly, the very first Congress passed the Alien Torts Statute, which grants the federal courts jurisdiction over any civil action by an alien for a wrongful act "committed in violation of the law of nations or a treaty of the United States." The exact scope of this statute has been controversial in terms of what kinds of wrongdoing are covered. That debate is beside the point for our purposes; what is important is that the Constitution explicitly refers to the law of nations, as did the first Congress (which included a number of the Framers of the Constitution).

As the modern Supreme Court has made clear, the first Congress assumed that federal courts could and would enforce international norms. Notably, the modern Court has also remarked that this understanding remains effective, notwithstanding the modern shift in views about the status of the common law. The Court explained that judges do not "lose all capacity to recognize enforceable international norms simply because the common law might lose some metaphysical cachet on the road to modern realism."[10]

Looking beyond our borders came naturally for the Framers. According to the Declaration of Independence, the whole reason for issuing this foundational document was based on a "decent Respect to the Opinions of Mankind." Early Americans, from Thomas Jefferson on down, understood that the law of nations was part of our legal system.

Early opinions of the Supreme Court were in accord with this view. Chief Justice Marshall, in a case with the whimsical name of *The Charming Betsy*,[11] proclaimed that federal laws "ought never to be construed to violate the law of nations if any other possible construction remains." Marshall also made it clear that, in the absence of legislation, the Supreme Court was "bound by the law of nations which is a part of the law of the land."[12] As Harold Koh, a distinguished international law expert and dean of Yale Law School, has said, "the early Supreme Court saw the judicial branch as a central channel for making international law part of U.S. law."[13] "Like it or not," he adds, "both foreign and international law are already part of our law."[14]

Today, the right of U.S. courts to consider foreign law is tremendously controversial. I will return to this issue for a more in-depth discussion later in the book. For present purposes, suffice it to say that the Framers had little doubt about the appropriateness of referring to the law of nations.

A New Idea: Using a Bill of Rights to Cement Natural Rights

While natural law was "in the air" in the Framing period, it might or might not have translated into hard restrictions on legislative power. Partly for this reason, perhaps, early state constitutions began to include express lists of rights. Such listings of rights had a long pedigree in England, stretching back to the Magna Charta in 1215 and the Bill of Rights of 1689.

The first American bill of rights came from Virginia. It covered rights such as freedom of the press, the free exercise of religion, limits on government searches, and even "the enjoyment of life and liberty, with the means . . . of pursuing and obtaining happiness and safety." Similarly, the Pennsylvania Declaration of Rights proclaimed that "all men are born equally free and independent, and have certain natural, inherent and inalienable rights." At a more specific level, among the concrete guarantees were free elections, protections for criminal defendants such as the right to confront witnesses, and freedom of speech and religion.

In contrast to the state constitutions, as we will see, the federal Constitution was proposed and ratified without any bill of rights. It did expressly protect a few specific rights, such as a ban on laws that impose criminal penalties retroactively, but rights received only passing attention in the midst of other provisions. Although the failure to include a bill of rights may have been partly inadvertent, once it was challenged, the Framers of the Constitution needed to come up with convincing justifications for their action. To understand the Ninth Amendment, we have to understand the arguments that they made during the ratification debate about the risks of including a bill of rights. Their point was that a bill of rights might be not only ineffective but positively harmful, if it led to a devaluation of whatever rights were not listed. The Ninth Amendment was in large part a response to that fear.

It is not surprising that there was confusion about the relationship between constitutional bills of rights and natural rights. The idea of natural rights was very old and established; written constitutions and their bills of rights were new and untried. Consequently, it took a while for the Framers to figure out how to make the two work in tandem.

3

The Debate over Whether to Have a Bill of Rights

The Ninth Amendment is like a message in a bottle from the Framers of the Constitution, revealing much about their perspective on human rights. Ironically, their viewpoint has little in common with today's self-proclaimed believers in the original understanding. Instead, they had a generous view of human rights.

Even those Framers who opposed the inclusion of a bill of rights in the Constitution did so because they felt that the rights were better protected in other ways. The drafting and ratification debates over the Constitution provide the backdrop for understanding the Ninth Amendment.

The failure to include a bill of rights in the original Constitution may have been a product of oversight and fatigue. There was so little discussion of the idea that it is hard to be sure of the reason for disregarding the issue. If it was an oversight, it turned out to be a serious blunder, because opponents of the Constitution made a major point of the lack of a bill of rights. In response to these criticisms, the supporters of the new Constitution spun off a series of arguments against the need for a bill of rights. One of the arguments that surfaced repeatedly was that it would be impossible to enumerate all of the rights and that leaving some out might be taken as a negative signal. This concern continued to play a role even after the Constitution's ratification, when Congress began to consider specific proposals for a bill of rights. The Ninth Amendment was a direct response to this concern.

A REMARKABLE OVERSIGHT: THE ABSENCE OF A FEDERAL BILL OF RIGHTS

From our point of view today, one of the most striking things about the Constitution as it went out for ratification was the almost complete absence of protection for individual rights. It did protect the right to habeas corpus, ban certain retroactive laws, and provide for juries in criminal cases. But it said nothing about religious freedom, freedom of the press, immunity from self-incrimination, and other constitutional rights that we have come to take for granted. We think of these guarantees as being at the heart of the Constitution, but originally they were not there at all.

Only near the end of the Convention did the issue of a bill of rights surface. But the suggestion to add a bill of rights was promptly rejected as soon as it arose, partly on the ground that it was unnecessary. This became a major issue in the campaign to ratify the Constitution. Anti-Federalists argued that a bill of rights was critical to prevent oppression by the new national government. Their arguments were to bear fruit later, but the Framers of the original Constitution did not initially accept their views.

If the Framers cared so much about natural rights, why did the Constitutional Convention of 1787 produce a document that had so little to say about them? The basic answer is that the drafters of the Constitution had other fish to fry. The original Constitution said almost nothing about individual rights because the Convention had focused on structural issues in creating a new national government.

The debates centered on such issues as whether to have a single president or a committee at the head of the government and how to elect members of Congress. Should states have equal representation in Congress, should they be represented on the basis of population, or should both forms of representation be used? Should the president be chosen by Congress or through some other mechanism? Who should be in charge of impeachment? How much power should Congress have to regulate? These were key issues in designing the new government, and the Convention struggled with how to resolve them until the end of the summer of 1787.

The first surfacing of the idea of a bill of rights in discussion was not auspicious. On August 20, 1787, Charles Pickney submitted a proposal to the Committee on Detail, but it was never heard from again. A soldier and prisoner of war during the Revolution, Pickney later became governor of South Carolina and a U.S. Senator. Pickney's proposal included freedom of the press and a ban on religious qualifications for office. The silence in response to his proposal was deafening.

In the last week of the Convention, George Mason raised the matter again, saying that a bill of rights would "give great quiet to the people; and with the aid of the State declarations, a bill might be prepared in a few hours." Mason was no lightweight but an influential writer who had helped frame the Declaration of Rights in Virginia. Eldridge Gerry, later Madison's vice president, made such a motion. (His surname later became the basis of the term "gerrymandered" because of a bizarre redistricting map.)

There was a brief and relatively unenlightening discussion of Gerry's motion. Roger Sherman spoke in opposition. He was a self-educated man whose writings nevertheless extended to astronomy, philosophy, and poetry; he had also been a judge and a member of the committee that drafted the Declaration of Independence. Sherman said that the states' bills of rights would remain in effect and provide sufficient protection.

The various arguments may have been a bit muddled because of the context. The specific issue under discussion was whether to guarantee jury trials in civil cases, and Sherman aptly pointed out that different states had very different rules on this question. He would later become an important player when Congress did get around to drafting a bill of rights, but for now he was unconvinced. In the end, not a single state voted in favor of Gerry's motion.

Two days later, Gerry raised the issue again. He and a South Carolina delegate moved "to insert a declaration 'that the liberty of the Press should be inviolably observed.'" Sherman was again opposed. His argument was that "the power of Congress does not extend to the Press." Hence, under Sherman's view, an endorsement of freedom of the press was unnecessary. The motion was defeated, though by a narrower margin than before.

Some of the supporters of a bill of rights then proposed that states should be allowed to propose amendments, which would then be considered in a new convention. This idea was roundly rejected as impractical. The Constitution was sent out to the Continental Congress for transmission to the states with no bill of rights.

THE BILL OF RIGHTS AND THE DEBATES OVER WHETHER TO ADOPT THE CONSTITUTION

The Convention might have done better to heed the objections. The absence of a bill of rights figured prominently in the debates over whether to ratify the Constitution. Mason himself refused to sign the Constitution and carried the fight to the states in the battle over ratification. His views were echoed by Patrick Henry, of "give me liberty or give me death" fame. Henry declaimed with his usual eloquence: "You have a bill of rights to defend you against the state government, which is bereaved of all power, and yet you have none against Congress, though in full and exclusive possession of all power!" "What barriers," he asked, "have you to oppose this most strong, energetic government?"

One of the leading opponents of the Constitution, who wrote under the name of "Brutus," made this objection most forcefully. (To this day, the true identity of Brutus is debated. Imagine a modern day "public intellectual" who was willing to forgo the publicity value of an important and popular series of publications!) Brutus argued that individuals retain many of their natural rights despite the social compact, such as the rights of conscience. Hence, in "forming a government on its true principles, the foundation should be laid . . . by expressly reserving to the people such of their essential natural rights, as are not necessary to be parted with."

Brutus referred to both English and American examples. In England, "magna charta and bill of rights have long been the boast, as well as to the security, of that nation." And in "all the constitutions of our own states; there is not one of them but what is founded on a declaration or bill of rights, or has certain express reservations of rights interwoven into the body of them." Brutus could not help but find it all "the more astonishing, that this grand security, to the rights of the people, is not to be found in this constitution."[1]

In defending their failure to provide a Bill of Rights, Federalists argued that doing so could actually backfire. They claimed that by listing *some* rights, a bill of rights would necessarily imply that the government's powers were otherwise unlimited. As an illustration of such reasoning, if a law says that "the police can carry weapons but not grenades and machetes," the implication is that all other weapons are allowed. Today, lawyers call this an *exclusio* argument (naming some things excludes all others), and this kind of argument is a particular favorite of conservatives like Justice Scalia. The Federalists argued that a partial enumeration of rights would carry a similar implication that those rights were exclusive. But any enumeration of rights would necessarily be incomplete. So the effect of a bill of rights would be to imperil every right that got left off the list. In short, what the Federalists were afraid of was that someone would use the listing of some rights as an excuse for trampling others.

For example, James Wilson (a leading figure among the Framers of the Constitution) thought it was ridiculous to try to enumerate all of human rights. Referring to European writers such as Pufendorf and Vattel, he said that they all "have treated on this subject; but in no one of those books, nor in the aggregate of them all, can you find a complete enumeration of rights appertaining to the people as men and as citizens."[2] He added caustically: "Enumerate all the rights of men! I am sure, sir, that no gentleman in the late Convention would have attempted such a thing."[3]

Later, Wilson explained that "if we attempt an enumeration, everything that is not enumerated is presumed to be given."[4] As a future Supreme Court Justice, James Iredell, said, it would "not only be useless, but dangerous" to enumerate rights, because "it would be implying in the strongest manner, that every right not included in the exception might be impaired by the government without usurpation; and it would be impossible to list them all." He challenged listeners to attempt such a listing and offered to identify twenty or thirty other rights that would have been overlooked. Apparently there were a lot of rights, not just a handful.[5]

The supporters of the Constitution mounted a number of arguments against the need for a bill of rights, but the absence of one was still a political liability. One problem was that the Constitution already contained some rights such as habeas corpus, which made the absence of other rights seem suspicious. Thus, as Jack Rakove explains, as "exaggerated as Anti-Federalist fears were, they confronted a theoretical problem of the first magnitude. Once a partial set of rights had received textual recognition as supreme law, did not that relegate all other rights to some lesser or more problematic status, even if they were originally derived from the variety of pre-existing sources to which the colonists had appealed before 1776?"[6]

THE MOVE TOWARD A FEDERAL BILL OF RIGHTS

Despite these arguments, the Federalists were forced to give up ground in this dispute. As part of the price of ratification, they promised to add a bill of rights after the Constitution went into effect. As soon as the new constitutional structure was in place, James Madison (the "Father of the Constitution" and later president) took the lead. Rakove, who has spent much of his career studying Madison, observes that "Madison's concerns with issues of rights can be traced to an early age."[7]

Virginia and other key states had ultimately ratified the Constitution, but they also sent Congress a list of proposed amendments. Notably, Virginia wanted an express constitutional proclamation of the need to protect natural rights, as did Rhode Island, South Carolina, and New York. The first of Virginia's proposals began as follows: "That there are certain natural rights of which men, when they form a social compact cannot deprive or divest their posterity."

Virginia and New York gave some added emphasis to their suggestions by proposing that a new convention be called, and two other states (North Carolina and Rhode Island) continued to reject the Constitution in part because it lacked a bill of rights. In response to these efforts, James Madison raised the issue in Congress after the first month of its initial session under the new Constitution. As much as he believed in rights, he had never been a strong believer in the utility of a bill of rights as a way of protecting them. However, he had finally come around to the view that it would be better to supply one.

By this time, however, the clamor for a bill of rights seems to have faded. Madison seems to have had difficulty getting Congress's attention. When he brought up the issue, there were immediate objections that he was wasting the House of Representatives' valuable time. More pressing matters, like establishing the federal judiciary and a tax system, needed attention. Some anti-Federalists actually resisted congressional consideration of a bill of rights, perhaps in the hope that a new constitutional convention might be called by disgruntled states. When Madison returned a month later to present his proposals, he began by apologizing for being "accessory to the loss of a single moment of time by the House."

When the Bill of Rights was under consideration, the argument once again surfaced that the universe of inalienable rights could not be usefully encompassed in a list. An interesting exchange took place in the First Congress on this issue. Representative Theodore Sedgwick objected to including the freedom of assembly in the Bill of Rights, on the ground that it was a "self-evident, unalienable right." He considered it demeaning for Congress to descend to such trivia.[8]

Sedgwick's remark gave rise to a spirited exchange. Another representative responded to Sedgwick by agreeing that the rights listed in the proposed constitutional amendments were inherent; the amendments were simply supposed to prevent the government from infringing them. Sedgwick replied that if *that* was what the drafters were doing, they would have needed a very long list indeed. Such a list would have to include a man's "right to wear his hat if he pleased; that he might get up when he pleased, and go to bed when he thought proper."[9] The response in turn was that "such rights have been opposed, and a man has been obligated to pull off his hat when he appeared before the face of authority," making it prudent to guard against such abuses by listing the rights.[10]

Such discussions on the floor of Congress confirmed the understanding that any list of rights would necessarily be incomplete. As a supporter of the Constitution had argued at the Pennsylvania ratification convention, "Our rights are not yet all known," so an enumeration was impossible.[11] Without a Ninth Amendment, the federal power might be able to invade every right that was not explicitly listed, and yet a complete list would be impossible. Thus, the Ninth Amendment addresses governmental invasions of privacy or human dignity that are not listed in the earlier amendment.

Joseph Story, one of the most influential Supreme Court Justices in the early years of the Republic, emphasized the link between the perceived impossibility of a comprehensive list of rights and the Ninth Amendment. He said the amendment was manifestly intended to prevent any "perverse or ingenious misapplication of the well-known maxim, that an affirmation in particular cases implies a negation in all others," a corollary of which was that providing explicit exceptions negated the existence of implicit ones.[12] It was Madison who came up with the Ninth Amendment as the solution to this problem.

4

Madison's Solution

We have finally come to the point where we can understand exactly what Madison was doing when he added the Ninth Amendment to the Bill of Rights. Madison gave a somewhat convoluted explanation of what he had in mind. His argument comes in several layers: an affirmative argument for a bill of rights, then a recital of the counterarguments against the bill of rights, accompanied by his rebuttals to those counterarguments, and finally explanations of his proposed amendments. With the Ninth Amendment, these layers are mixed together, because the reason *for* the Ninth Amendment is to counter one of the arguments *against* having a bill of rights at all. For this reason, Madison's explanation requires careful parsing.

One of the Federalist arguments against a bill of rights had been that federal power was too limited to require such protections. But when he brought forward the Bill of Rights, Madison admitted that this might not be the case. The Necessary and Proper Clause gave Congress wide discretion over the use of means to exercise its constitutional powers, and Congress might abuse that discretion by invading individual rights. For example, Congress had the power to collect revenue, just like the old British government. The Necessary and Proper Clause gives Congress discretion over the means to use in seeking that goal. Might it not use the same unbounded search warrants that the British had adopted for this purpose?

The supporters of the Constitution had previously tried to defuse this argument. They argued that Congress's powers were not really broad enough to threaten human rights. At one level, this argument was plainly misguided. Congress's powers included control over interstate commerce, authority over military matters, the ability to tax citizens, and a sweeping authorization to pass whatever laws were "necessary and proper" to exercise those and other powers. These powers were certainly great enough that their abuse could be a threat to liberty. On the other hand, a good eighteenth-century lawyer could have come up with some arguments for viewing these congressional powers in a different light. For example, the Necessary and Proper Clause could be construed to include respect for natural rights as part of the definition of what laws are "proper."

Notwithstanding the possibility that courts might defuse some of the risk through interpretation of congressional powers, the powers of the federal government were great enough to pose a potential threat to human rights, which might require more security than the vague hope that courts would recognize implicit limits on those powers. Madison was now prepared to concede this point, though he had not been during the earlier debates over ratifying the Constitution.

Although Madison no longer seemed to take very seriously the argument that Congress's powers were too limited to pose a threat, he remained troubled by the risk that the effect of a bill of rights might be to exclude whatever rights failed to make the final list. The Ninth Amendment was intended to counter this risk.

Madison's major speech on the proposal directly addressed the exclusivity problem. He recognized the risk—which has played out in an all-too real way among today's conservatives—that any attempt to list fundamental rights in the Bill of Rights would be mistakenly read to undermine the legal status of other rights. Madison called this "one of the most plausible arguments I have ever heard urged against the admission of a bill of rights into this system."

Certainly, natural rights were very much on the minds of Madison and his fellow legislators. In his notes for the speech introducing the Bill of Rights, Madison had underlined the term "natural rights" as part of his categorization of different kinds of rights.[1] His thinking had no doubt evolved over the years, but he still retained his belief in the existence of these rights.

After being lost for two centuries, the notes of another member of the congressional drafting committee surfaced in the 1980s. The committee member in question was none other than Roger Sherman, who had opposed the idea of a bill of rights at the Constitutional Convention of 1787. As his notes show, by the time of the First Congress, Sherman was now on board to the extent of doing a little drafting of his own. His version of the Bill of Rights began with a statement that the people have certain natural rights and then went on to provide a list of them, including religious freedom and free speech.

Madison's response to the exclusivity problem was different from Sherman's. While Sherman had included an endorsement of the general concept of natural rights, Madison focused more directly on the problem of exclusivity. He proposed the following provision to deal with the exclusivity issue:

> *The exceptions here or elsewhere in the Constitution, made in favor of particular rights, shall not be so construed as to diminish the just importance of other rights retained by the people*, or as to enlarge the powers delegated by the Constitution; but either as actual limitations of such powers, or as inserted merely for greater security.

The first part of this provision, which I have italicized here, became the basis for the Ninth Amendment. The second part disappeared before the Bill of Rights left the House of Representatives.

We need to take a careful look at Madison's language, including both the parts that were ultimately adopted and those that were dropped. The proposal that Madison presented to Congress provides clear signs about the Framers' intent regarding unenumerated rights.

There are several things to notice about Madison's proposal. First, he refers to the unenumerated rights as *other* rights retained by the people. This reference comes just after he refers to the express constitutional rights of the Bill of Rights. Also, the Constitution is described as making exceptions in favor of certain rights, not as creating those rights. The implication is that both sets of rights—explicit and implied—are retained, meaning that all of those rights already existed and were merely being kept in place. Thus, both enumerated and unenumerated rights are similar in their origins; neither kind is "created" by the Constitution or the Bill of Rights.

Second, notice the deleted language saying that enumerated rights do not indirectly expand other federal powers. The deletion of this language is significant because it disproves one misreading of the Ninth Amendment, which tries to twist it into an effort to restrict federal powers rather than to recognize unenumerated rights. If the idea was to restrict federal power, that language was there as part of Madison's draft. The fact that this specific language was deleted shows that the remaining language had a different purpose.

Third, Madison proposed this language as part of his fifth block of amendments, which also contained the basis for what would later become the first eight amendments, protecting rights to free speech, against self-incrimination and unreasonable searches, and so forth. In Madison's original proposal, rather than being placed at the end, each of the amendments would have been inserted somewhere in the original text of the 1789 Constitution—in this case right after the guarantee of habeas corpus and the ban on bills of attainder and ex post facto laws. Thus, Madison was clearly thinking of rights of the same kind in terms of the Ninth Amendment.

As he said in his main speech about the Bill of Rights, Madison had in mind "rights which are retained when particular powers are given up to be exercised by the Legislature," along with other rights such as jury trial "as essential to secure the liberty of the people as any one of the pre-existent rights of nature." The placement of the Ninth Amendment language along with these individual rights was the same in the next draft, issued by the House Select Committee on July 28, 1789.

When the Ninth Amendment emerged from the House committee, Madison's reference to "exceptions made in favor of particular rights" had been changed to the final language, "the enumeration in this Constitution of certain rights." The use of the word "enumeration" is significant. Enumeration means to number or list; it doesn't mean to create. For example, the Constitution also uses this term to refer to the census, which obviously lists items (in this case people) that already exist beforehand.

Significantly, the House Committee didn't use other terms such as "establish," "ordain," or "enact" in speaking of the rights listed in the Constitution. The Committee might, for example, have referred to "rights granted by this Constitution" or "rights ordained and established by this Constitution." Clearly these were all familiar terms; they were used in other parts of the Constitution. According to the Preamble, "We the People . . . ordain and establish" the Constitution. Congress is also authorized to "ordain and establish" the lower federal courts. And Article I says that the powers of Congress are "herein granted" and "vested" in Congress. But rights seemingly are not granted, established, or ordained by the Constitution, nor does the Constitution vest rights in individuals; rights (or rather, some of them) are simply *listed* there.

Sometimes, the Ninth Amendment is thought to be about limiting federal power in the interest of state's rights. Notably, Madison made a different proposal relating to states' rights, which became what is now the Tenth Amendment. That proposal stated that the "powers not delegated by this Constitution, nor prohibited by it to the States, are reserved to the States respectively." This amendment was not part of the fifth block (which contained the future Ninth Amendment). Instead, it was part of the eighth block of amendments in Madison's speech. Madison proposed to insert it in an entirely different part of the Constitution, just after Article VI (rather than Article I).

Madison's explanation and the accompanying proposals make his intentions unmistakable. The proposal that became the Ninth Amendment was not paired with the future Tenth Amendment. It was not about federalism; it was about individual rights. Those individual rights belonged to the same genre as free speech (in the proposed Bill of Rights) or the ban on ex post facto law (in the original Constitution). Explicitly listing rights had advantages, in terms of both reassuring the public and stimulating judges to come more readily to their defense. But Madison had done as much as he could to communicate that the listing was not exclusive: there were other important rights, and they too were entitled to respect even though they were not specifically enumerated.

5

After the Ninth

After the Ninth Amendment was in place, you might have expected it and the rest of the Bill of Rights to become focal points for American legal development. The fact that this did not happen is the first of several surprising twists in our story.

A Case of Constitutional Amnesia

If the meaning of the Ninth Amendment was so clear, why do I need to write a book to prove my case? Why isn't my view already the law?

The problem is that the Ninth Amendment went into hibernation almost as soon as it was created. Unlike the other amendments, it was not a direct response to state-level clamor for a federal bill of rights. Thus, it lacked a preexisting constituency. If the First Congress had legislated broadly on personal matters such as marriage or childbearing, the Ninth Amendment might have become politically salient. But as it turned out, politics in the early republic revolved around other issues, to which the Ninth Amendment was not very relevant. Indeed, the Bill of Rights as a whole made only a sporadic appearance in political debate.

The Ninth Amendment was based on a fear that federal regulation would intrude on individual liberties. As it turned out, while the Federalist Party was in power, the main threats to liberty were the infamous Alien and Sedition Laws, which were targeted at the Jeffersonian critics of Hamilton and his allies. These laws so clearly violated the First Amendment that there was no reason to think about unenumerated rights.

After the Federalists were replaced by the Jeffersonians and Jacksonians, the federal government did very little in terms of regulation. It seemed to be doing its best to live up to the Federalist pre-ratification argument that it would be too weak to pose any danger to liberty. When a government refuses to exercise its powers, we do not need to invoke rights guarantees to prevent overreaching.

In their reaction against Hamilton and the Federalist Party's platform, Southerners like Jefferson and Madison developed a constitutional theory that stressed states' rights and strict construction of federal powers. Even using federal money to build roads or improve waterways became hugely controversial. When it was mentioned at all, the Ninth Amendment was often erroneously lumped together with the Tenth Amendment (which preserves the "powers retained by the states") as a guarantee of states' rights. States' rights were the issue of the day, an issue so explosive that it eventually blossomed into civil war.

After the Federalist Party lost power, Congress did relatively little in the way of regulation until the Civil War. Thus, there was no reason to raise the Ninth Amendment as a defense to federal regulation, and correspondingly no reason for the federal courts to hear any Ninth Amendment cases. The Ninth Amendment faded from view. It was only in the late nineteenth century, with the birth of the modern regulatory state, that individual rights again became a central issue, but by that time the Ninth Amendment was nearly forgotten.

Indeed, the Bill of Rights as a whole received little attention from the federal courts for much of the nineteenth century. In the sixty years between Jefferson's election and Lincoln's, provisions such as the First Amendment's guarantee of free speech or the Fourth

Amendment's protection against unreasonable searches received only sporadic mention from the Supreme Court (usually about once a decade and often as just part of a laundry list of individual rights). It was not until the early twentieth century that the First Amendment was actually enforced by the Supreme Court.

In a world where the express guarantees of the Bill of Rights did not count for much, it is no wonder that the Ninth Amendment was ignored. Indeed, you could argue that the Court was scrupulously complying with the Ninth Amendment by treating unenumerated rights with complete equality to enumerated ones—and ignoring them both almost completely.

This amnesia was to have unfortunate consequences. When the Supreme Court did turn to the protection of fundamental rights in the late nineteenth century, it had completely forgotten about the Ninth Amendment. This, plus another historical quirk that we will discuss later, led the Court to rely on a dubious textual basis for protecting fundamental rights. As a result, its efforts have been under shadow ever since, with persistent doubts about whether the whole enterprise of judicial protection of fundamental rights was legitimate.

FUNDAMENTAL RIGHTS IN NINETEENTH-CENTURY LAW

The Ninth Amendment may have been forgotten, but not the ideas for which it stood. The idea of natural rights remained important in contexts other than defending against national legislation. As we will see, judges as well as important political figures continued to think in terms of natural rights well after the adoption of the Ninth Amendment. The Ninth Amendment itself may have slipped their minds, yet its underlying rationale remained vibrant.

Although the Ninth Amendment faded from view, natural law and the law of nations remained prominent in American thought well after the framing of the Constitution, right up to the Civil War. They played a role in legal decisions and, equally important, in the thinking that led to fundamental constitutional amendment during Reconstruction.

The continuing vitality of natural law shows that it was not merely a phenomenon of the Revolutionary period; it had enough staying power to influence the Fourteenth Amendment "four score and seven years" later. A review of early judicial decisions confirms that natural law continued to play an important role in American law well into the nineteenth century. I mentioned in chapter 1 Justice Chase's opinion in *Calder v. Bull*,[1] in which he proclaimed that state governments were limited by "certain vital principles in our free Republican governments, which will determine and overrule an apparent and flagrant abuse of legislative power."

Chief Justice Marshall was a far more influential judge, and he was also sympathetic toward this same position. In *Fletcher v. Peck*,[2] for instance, not content to rest on the contract clause, he also relied on "general principles which are common to our free institutions."[3] A number of state court decisions asserted a similar view in the earlier part of the nineteenth century.

Natural law theories were also adopted by commentators during this period. For example, the great judge and scholar Chancellor Kent maintained that the rights of personal security, liberty, and property were "natural, inherent, and unalienable." Drawing on the theories of natural law writers like Pufendorf, Kent held that the power of the legislature to take private property was limited by principles of natural equity. Natural law concepts also found expression by notable lawyers in their briefs and arguments before judges.

Salmon Chase (a future U.S. Chief Justice) gave one of the clearest expositions of these principles in a lengthy court argument. He said that the Bill of Rights was designed to establish as written law some of the great principles of natural law that exist independently of such enactments. The Bill of Rights did not create restrictions that the legislator would otherwise be free to ignore in its absence. Instead, it merely announced restrictions on legislative power deriving from the nature of society and government. These restrictions apply universally to all governments, according to Chase: no legislature is omnipotent, nor can a legislature make right into wrong any more than it can change light into darkness—and no legislature can make human beings into things, mere chattels in the way that slave law purported to do.

Nor were these merely moral maxims that should guide the legislative process. They applied to courts as well, said the future Chief Justice. He held that no court is bound to enforce unjust law; on the contrary, judges are bound to abstain from enforcing such laws. He added that it "must be a clear case, doubtless, which will warrant a court in pronouncing a law so unjust that it ought not to be enforced; but, in a clear case, the path of duty is plain."[4]

The persistence of natural law in judicial opinions and treatises was notable, but ultimately less important than its influence on the emerging antislavery movement. Natural law pervaded the thinking of antislavery Republicans, who later brought forth the Fourteenth Amendment. They were animated by the same vision of human rights that inspired the Framers. Building on the Ninth and the rest of the Bill of Rights, the Fourteenth subjected state governments to constitutional limitations, requiring them to provide due process and equal protection of the law and forbidding them from violating the "privileges or immunities" of U.S. citizenship.

THE CONSTITUTION'S NEARLY FATAL FLAW: ELUDING THE ISSUE OF SLAVERY

There were only two constitutional amendments between the Bill of Rights and the Civil War. One of them modified the original, deeply flawed system for electing the president, which had almost wrecked the country with a tie in the election of 1800; the other protected states from being sued for damages in federal court after a contrary ruling from the Supreme Court. At that point, it may have seemed the constitutional structure was more or less complete. Once the basic structure of government was in place, however, the key flaw in the original constitutional scheme became more and more troubling. The Constitution had dodged the issue of slavery, providing some protections to the slave states but carefully avoiding any explicit reference to slaves. This was an increasingly unstable compromise between a document that promised the "blessings of Liberty" and an institution dedicated to the annihilation of freedom.

The slavery question was repeatedly brought back on the national agenda because of events relating to the country's western expansion. In 1819, controversy erupted over the admission of Missouri to the union. The outcome was another compromise. Except in Missouri itself, slavery would be allowed only below the line of Missouri's southern border. The annexation of Texas and the Mexican war brought the slavery issue back to the political forefront. In the course of the war, a congressional debate on slavery had erupted over the Wilmot Proviso, which would have banned slavery in any territory that might be acquired from Mexico. Although it never passed, the Wilmot Proviso reopened the slavery issue in national politics.

For the next ten years, the nation was plagued by disputes over the status of slavery in the territories. The 1850 Compromise engineered by Henry Clay and Daniel Webster (with the crucial help of Stephen Douglas) seemed for a time to quiet the dispute. It admitted California as a free state, established territorial governments in the rest of the territory acquired from Mexico, and (most ominously) enacted a new Fugitive Slave Law. Many Americans thought this compromise had put the slavery issue to rest.

Events were to prove them wrong. As a by-product of his plans to build a transcontinental railroad, Douglas proposed the Kansas-Nebraska Act, which opened territories to slavery where it had not been allowed under the earlier Missouri Compromise. This statute exploded the relative calm that had prevailed after the 1850 Compromise. The resulting turmoil earned the territory the nickname "Bleeding Kansas" and also polarized Congress. And not least, it galvanized Abraham Lincoln to reenter the political fray in a crusade against the spread of slavery.

Enforcement of the fugitive slave laws encountered increasingly violent Northern resistance. As antislavery forces became more powerful in the North, proslavery forces in the South became more extreme, advocating slavery in the territories, annexation of new territory in Latin America, and reopening the international slave trade. By the end of the 1850s, the slavery issue had seemingly passed any hope of compromise, and talk of secession was rampant. The Supreme Court had not helped the situation with its 1857 *Dred Scott* decision, which held that blacks could never become citizens and that Congress lacked any power to ban slavery in the territories. In the run up to the election of 1860, the Democratic Party fractured under the stress of the slavery issue, leaving only regional parties to contest the election.

In 1860, Lincoln was elected president with only a plurality of the national popular vote but a majority in the electoral college. By the end of the following month, a South Carolina state convention had voted to secede, and the stage was set for civil war. The Constitution's greatest time of crisis was at hand, and it would result in the most important constitutional changes since the Bill of Rights. Before we turn to the constitutional amendments that emerged from the war, however, we need to understand the intellectual perspective of the men who wrote and adopted these provisions.

6

Natural Law and the Antislavery Republicans

In pre–Civil War America, the Framers were not distant historical figures but a looming presence. The antislavery Republicans were much closer in time to the Framers than we are to either group. When Lincoln took office, James Madison had been dead for only twenty-six years. This is about as much time as has elapsed between the publication of this book and the election of Ronald Reagan. When Lincoln referred to the founding of the nation "four score and seven years" earlier, he was referring to a single human life span. (For comparison, four score and seven years before the writing of this book would be the early 1920s, about the year my father was born.) It is little wonder that the ideas of the Declaration of Independence resonated so deeply with Lincoln and his generation.

Of course, much had changed in politics and the economy since the Founding. But it is not surprising that major threads of Founding-era thought remained largely intact. Like the Framers, Civil War–era Republicans were attempting to recreate a sound governmental structure and protect basic rights in the aftermath of a bloody war. It is not surprising that the Ninth Amendment and the Fourteenth Amendment—which was ratified seventy-seven years after the Ninth—have a great deal in common. Nor is it surprising that, more than 200 years after the Ninth and 140 years after the Fourteenth, we have lost some important historical memory about their meanings. Ideas from the Founding era that were still in the air before the Civil War now have to be recovered through patient historical research.

NATURAL LAW AND THE ANTISLAVERY REPUBLICANS

In the period before the Civil War, antislavery Republicans adamantly defended the concept of natural law. Consider the views of Senator William Seward, who proclaimed in a famous antislavery speech that there was a higher law than the Constitution.[1] Seward was no extremist ideologue. He was the most important member of the Republican Party other than Lincoln, and had been the frontrunner for the Republican nomination before Lincoln seized the lead. He served as Secretary of State for eight years.

In the key passage of his "higher law" speech, Seward said that Congress held no power of arbitrary action over the new territories. He also explained that slavery was incompatible with natural rights. Elsewhere, he proclaimed that the Constitution gave Congress no power to deprive men of their natural rights and inalienable liberty.[2] Seward's views were echoed by other leading Republicans like Benjamin Wade and Charles Sumner.

John Bingham, who later played the leading role in drafting the Fourteenth Amendment, replied vigorously to criticisms of the higher law theory. It is worth hearing just what the author of the Fourteenth Amendment had to say about natural law. He began by stating that he knew his attack on slavery would be "met with the sneer that this is the 'higher law.'" But, he said, the higher law was part of the American tradition: "Pray, did not Madison recognize a higher law when, in the convention of 1787, he declared that it was *WRONG* to admit in the Constitution that there can be property in man?" "No, sir," Bingham proclaimed, the Founding Fathers never would have "borne the sacred ark of liberty through a seven years' war, if they had not believed in a higher law—in the eternal verities of truth and justice." For Bingham, natural law was "of perpetual and of universal obligation"—"obligatory alike upon individual and collective man; upon the citizen and upon the State."[3]

For moderates like Abraham Lincoln, belief in natural law did not imply immunity from the duties imposed by legislation, even if that legislation violated natural law. For example, Lincoln maintained that if elected to Congress, it would be his duty to pass legislation enforcing the Fugitive Slave Clause. For him, natural law was like the law of nations, filling gaps in the law but capable of being displaced by legislation. He believed that slavery violated the law of nations but that Southern slave legislation had legal effect in the states where it had been adopted. However, in the Territories, where there was no slave legislation, the law of nations remained in effect, and slavery was illegal.

Others took a stricter view of the commands of natural law. John Hale, the first openly antislavery candidate elected to the Senate, argued that a jury was no more obliged to give effect to a law recognizing slavery than it would to a law recognizing ownership of moonbeams. Of the fugitive slave law, Joshua Giddings declared that no one could say there was no higher law than this legislation, and he vowed to resist its enforcement.[4] Giddings went so far as to defend an uprising and murder by slaves aboard the slave ship *Creole*. Far from being an outbreak of lawless violence, he said, the slaves' rebellion "asserted the rights bestowed upon them by the Creator."[5]

RENEWING THE FRAMERS' VISION
OF NATURAL LAW

For many Republicans, the wellsprings of natural law were to be found with the Founding Fathers. The Republicans went to great lengths to demonstrate the Fathers' antislavery sentiments. As Wade once said, "I do not understand that . . . I claim anything more than was claimed by the founders of this Republic. I am not the advocate of any new doctrine. I stand upon the principles of the fathers of our Constitution."[6]

Based on the statements of the Framers, the constitutional debates, and the Federalist Papers, Seward stated the basic Republican position that the Constitution did not endorse slavery but left that question to the law of nature and of nations. "That law," he said, "as expounded by Vattel, is founded in the reason of things."[7] Note the reference to Vattel—apparently, the founders of the Republican Party were more cosmopolitan than their present-day successors in terms of their willingness to cite foreign legal authorities.

Similarly, in an 1858 speech, Senator Howard (who later introduced the Fourteenth Amendment to the Senate) collected antislavery statements from Founding Fathers such as Jefferson, Patrick Henry, James Monroe, John Randolph, and others. In another 1858 speech, Hale cited opinions by Jefferson, Patrick Henry, William Pinckney, and John Jay.

The Declaration of Independence may have been the most important source of inspiration for antislavery Republicans, and thanks to Jefferson it embodies the views of Enlightenment thinkers like Locke and Vattel. Today, the Declaration does not get much attention from lawyers and probably not much attention from anyone else outside of high school history classes and Fourth of July speeches. Antislavery Republicans like Lincoln, however, took a decidedly different view. They considered the Declaration to be part of the law of nations and a cornerstone of American law.

Adherence to the Declaration became a kind of touchstone for Republicans. In the 1860 platform, the party officially affirmed its belief in the "the principles promulgated in the Declaration of Independence and embodied in the Federal Constitution," and the Republican platform then quoted the key passage from the Declaration about equality and inalienable rights. This provision was not boilerplate, included out of a sort of ceremonial piety. Instead, it was adopted out of parliamentary order when Giddings threatened a walkout unless it was accepted—members of the party thought that reaffirming the Declaration was *that* important.

This 1860 platform comported well with Lincoln's views. Lincoln himself steered away from explicit references to "higher law" that might alienate moderates. Yet the core of his creed was the Declaration of Independence, with its central premise that all people are created equal and endowed with certain inalienable rights.

In the Lincoln-Douglas debates, Lincoln had continually taunted Stephen Douglas about Douglas's unfaithfulness to the Declaration. Douglas believed that people had only the rights the law chose to provide them. For blacks, of course, that meant no rights at all, unless a particular state or territorial government chose to abolish slavery. For Lincoln, this stingy view of human rights was unacceptable. He repeatedly stressed the Declaration in his debates with Douglas, who insisted that it was never meant to apply to African Americans. In one speech, for example, Lincoln said, "I adhere to the Declaration of Independence. If Judge Douglas and his friends are not willing to stand by it, let them come up and amend it. Let them make it read that all men are created equal except negroes. Let us have it decided whether the Declaration of Independence, in this blessed year of 1858, shall be thus amended."[8] Lincoln exclaimed in another debate that "if the Declaration is not the truth, let us get the statute book, in which we find it, and tear it out!"[9] He used this attack on Douglas again and again in the debates, insisting that Douglas was distorting the meaning of the Declaration by adopting a reading that not a single person had ever endorsed until a few years earlier.

In a less obvious but vitally important way, Lincoln later reaffirmed his view of the centrality of the Declaration of Independence in the Gettysburg Address. There, Lincoln harkened back to the founding of the nation "four score and seven years ago"—meaning 1776, not 1789, when the Constitution was adopted. Echoing the language of the Declaration, he said that the nation was founded on the proposition that "all men are created equal," and he ended his speech with a call for a new birth of freedom like that of the Revolutionary War generation. From beginning to end, Lincoln held to the Declaration's pronouncements as the keystone of the American national identity.

Lincoln's views are particularly significant, not only because of who he was but because he spoke for many others. His fight for the Republican nomination was successful because of his acceptability to all factions of the party. Because he was at the party's center, historians view him as an example of the thinking of average Republicans. Although he was unique in many respects, he was far from unusual among Republicans in his basic philosophy.

In short, the Declaration of Independence rested on a view about natural rights that had broad appeal to Republicans, who rarely had much reason to specify exactly what rights were protected by natural law. The black slaves who were the object of their antislavery campaign had essentially no rights at all. Hence, there was little reason to try to enumerate just what rights were denied the slaves— name a right, and slaves didn't have it.

Thus, even before the Civil War, the Republicans had a well-developed conception of natural law, resting firmly in the Declaration of Independence and its natural law tradition. What they lacked was the ability to bridge the gap between their aspirations for a just legal order and the realities of antebellum society. The Civil War was to change all of that.

7

A New Birth of Freedom

As we have seen, a powerful wing of the Republican Party embraced the concept of natural law. What makes the antislavery Republicans so important is that they fathered three crucial constitutional amendments: the Thirteenth (ending slavery), the Fourteenth (providing federal guarantees against state violations of basic rights), and the Fifteenth (giving blacks the right to vote). In the end, the Republicans did not just preach about fundamental rights; they gave those rights a firm constitutional foundation.

The Amendment that has turned out to have the most lasting utility is the Fourteenth. Except among lawyers, the term "Fourteenth Amendment" is not in common use, in contrast to the First Amendment, which is often used by non-lawyers to refer to its rights of freedom of speech and religion. ("Taking the Fifth" also used to be a common phrase, meaning that a person was invoking the Fifth Amendment right against self-incrimination.) Hence, for readers who are not familiar with constitutional law, it is worth pausing for a moment to describe the amendment in more detail.

There are five sections of the Fourteenth Amendment, but only the first section and the last have had any continuing importance. They read as follows (with added italics of some key phrases):

Section 1. All Persons born or naturalized in the United States, and subject to the jurisdiction thereof, are citizens of the United States and of the State where they reside. No State shall make or enforce any law which shall abridge the *privileges or immunities* of citizens of the United States; nor shall any State deprive any person of life, liberty, or property, without *due process* of law; nor deny to any person within its jurisdiction the *equal protection* of the laws. . . .

Section 5. The Congress shall have power to *enforce*, by appropriate legislation, the provisions of this article.

About 90 percent of the Supreme Court's constitutional decisions directly or indirectly involve this language. Since the 1791 Bill of Rights only limits the power of the *federal* government to violate rights, any case today involving a state violation of rights comes under the Fourteenth Amendment. The Fourteenth Amendment came after Republicans had already spent a considerable time discussing the relationship between the Constitution and national rights. We need to start with the earliest phase of that discussion, the debate over the Thirteenth Amendment.

THE THIRTEENTH AMENDMENT AND THE END OF SLAVERY

The first opportunity for the Republicans to put some of their theories into the Constitution came with the Thirteenth Amendment. Today, the Thirteenth Amendment is only rarely the basis for lawsuits or legislation, but the Fourteenth Amendment is difficult to understand without first understanding the Thirteenth.

By mid-1863, Republicans were ready for a definitive solution to the slavery problem. Lincoln's Emancipation Proclamation was fine as far as it went, but it did not cover the entire country, and no one knew whether it would have any continuing legal effect after the war ended. Most Republicans had become convinced that abolition was necessary to ensure the Union's future security. In their minds, slavery and rebellion had become one. And the only way to abolish the institution itself was through a constitutional amendment.

The Thirteenth Amendment provides that "neither slavery nor involuntary servitude, except as a punishment for crime whereof the party shall have been duly convicted, shall exist within the United States, or any place subject to their jurisdiction." Section 2 gives Congress the power to enforce the Amendment "by appropriate legislation." This grant of congressional enforcement power was not found in earlier amendments, but it has been copied in most later ones, including the Fourteenth.

As they had before the Civil War, opponents of slavery looked to the Declaration of Independence for support as they debated the Thirteenth Amendment. A notable instance was provided by Maryland Senator Reverdy Johnson. A particularly cool-headed legal thinker, rarely given to rhetorical flights, Johnson was also far from being a zealous abolitionist; he had actually represented the slave owner in the famous *Dred Scot* case. Johnson said: "We mean that the Government in future shall be as it has been in the past, . . . an example of human freedom for the light and example of the world, and illustrating in the blessings and the happiness it confers the truth of the principles incorporated into the Declaration of Independence, that life and liberty are man's inalienable right."[1]

Lyman Trumbull, the influential moderate Republican senator from Illinois, also noted the inconsistency between the Declaration, which proclaimed the equal rights of all to life, liberty, and happiness, and the denial of liberty, happiness, and life itself to a whole race.[2]

Among those who made more direct appeals to higher law, one outspoken member of the House favored the Thirteenth Amendment because it would "secure to the oppressed slave his natural and God-given rights." Among those inalienable rights, he said, were the right to live, to enjoy the fruit of his own labor, and the "right to the endearments and enjoyment of family ties."[3] The reference to family ties should not be overlooked. One of the great evils of slavery was the way it broke up families, and Republicans must have had this in mind as one of the inalienable rights denied to slaves.

The debates on the Thirteenth Amendment are full of references to natural law. Another member of the House argued that no constitution could ever legalize the enslavement of men.[4] Yet another pronounced that legislation establishing slavery contravenes "the law of natural justice, and cannot establish a claim which 'white men are bound to respect'"—the last phrase being a bitter reference to Chief Justice Taney's infamous dictum in *Dred Scot* that black people had no rights that "white men are bound to respect."

The Debates on the Civil Rights Bill of 1866

In the immediate aftermath of the Civil War, Southern governments were dominated by leading Confederates. Even more disturbing were the new black codes in the Southern states, which restricted the rights of blacks severely. These laws were little more than attempts by the Southern states to restore slavery in a more subtle form. Congressional Republicans were now convinced of the need for additional guarantees to protect blacks in the South. They

were also concerned about the treatment of white Union sympa-
thizers in the South, who had been subject to widespread reprisals.

When Congress convened at the end of 1865, moderate Republicans immediately went about formulating a new plan for Reconstruction. Senator Trumbull of Illinois, who chaired the Senate
Judiciary Committee, introduced the Civil Rights bill in the Senate
in early 1866. It was designed to undo the Southern black codes. To
the dismay of congressional Republicans, President Andrew Johnson vetoed the Civil Rights bill. He contended that the matters covered by the bill were within the exclusive jurisdiction of the states,
and that the bill was thus unconstitutional. Both houses of Congress voted to override the veto.

The rhetoric of the debates over the Civil Rights bill had evolved
somewhat from the language used to discuss the Thirteenth
Amendment. The focus changed from the language of natural
rights to the language of citizenship. Many Republicans did com-
ment that the bill was designed to protect natural rights belonging
to all human beings. However, they more often referred to these
rights in the later debates as belonging to U.S. citizens.

For present purposes, the Civil Rights Act is mostly important because of the ideas surfacing during the debates about it. In the Senate, Trumbull argued that "the rights of a citizen of the United
States were certain great fundamental rights, such as the right to
life, to liberty, and to avail one's self of all the laws passed for the
benefit of the citizen to enable him to enforce his rights." As a basis
for defining those rights, Trumbull relied on a decision construing a
fairly obscure part of the 1789 Constitution.

The Privileges and Immunities Clause (known to lawyers as the P
and I Clause) prohibits states from depriving citizens of other states
of their privileges and immunities. This clause has a narrow interpretation today but was given a broader reading then, with antislavery Republicans taking an especially enthusiastic view of its scope.

This clause had been interpreted by Justice Bushrod Washington, George Washington's nephew, to protect fundamental rights. In his ruling on the *Corfield* case, he had held that the clause protects rights which are "in their nature, fundamental; which belong, of right, to the citizens of all free governments; and which have, at all times, been enjoyed by the citizens of the several states." Justice Washington had included among these rights: "protection by the government; the enjoyment of life and liberty, with the right to acquire and possess property of every kind, and to pursue and obtain happiness and safety."[5] Although they were subject to legitimate regulation, this was still a broad range of rights, not exactly a Scalia-like view of constitutional law. Trumbull found this a useful definition of fundamental rights. Given that these privileges and immunities already attached to citizenship under the P and I Clause, he reasoned that after Congress granted the former slaves citizenship, "the same rights would then appertain to all persons who were clothed with American citizenship."[6]

In the House, Representative Wilson argued that the rights protected in the bill were not new because they were already contained in the P and I Clause as construed in *Corfield*. In his view, that clause represented a "general citizenship" that "entitles every citizen to security and protection of personal rights."[7] Speaking at great length, another member of the House maintained that Congress had the power to secure citizens "in the enjoyment of their inherent right of life, liberty, and property," based on the P and I Clause.[8]

Another concept about the rights of citizens played an important role in the debates. Republicans argued that there is an implicit quid pro quo: citizens owe allegiance to their government in exchange for the government's grant of protection to them. Thus, one of the most important rights of citizenship is the right to receive such protection. This right to government protection served as a source of federal authority to defend the rights of citizens, whether those rights directly derived from the law of nations or from the P and I Clause.

After President Johnson's veto, Senator Trumbull made an important speech in the Senate defending the bill against Johnson's charges. He asserted that to "be a citizen of the United States carries with it some rights," namely "those inherent, fundamental rights which belong to free citizens or free men in all countries." In short, Trumbull emphasized, "the right of American citizenship means something." What American citizenship meant was government protection for "inalienable rights, belonging to every citizen of the United States, as such, no matter where he may be."[9]

THE FOURTEENTH AMENDMENT

This brings us, finally, to the crux of the post–Civil War enactments, the Fourteenth Amendment. The Civil Rights Act had attempted to provide statutory protection for fundamental rights in the South. Whether Congress really had the constitutional power to do so was subject to some dispute. Legislation such as the Civil Rights Act had another flaw. If the Republicans lost their grip on power, Democrats might easily repeal the legislation and leave blacks to the not-so-tender mercies of Southern whites. The Fourteenth Amendment was meant to address these threats.

Perversely, abolishing slavery actually threatened to increase the political power of Southern whites. Under the original Constitution, seats in the House were apportioned according to population, with slaves counting for this purpose as only three-fifths of a person. With the abolition of slavery, this provision was inoperative, so the South actually stood to gain representation. There was a clear argument for locking in some of the key elements of Reconstruction by giving them constitutional status. This was the goal behind the Fourteenth Amendment.

The first section of the Fourteenth Amendment has turned out to be the most important. It prohibited states from violating due process, equal protection, and the "privileges or immunities of citizens of the United States." The theory behind this section was that states should have respected human rights on the basis of the existing Constitution, but that they had failed to do so. Hence, the federal government needed new powers in order to force them to do so.

Two weeks after Congress overrode Johnson's veto of the Civil Rights Act, Representative Stevens placed before the joint committee a new Reconstruction plan. One aspect of the plan was a proposed constitutional amendment.[10] After some maneuvering in committee, Senator Bingham successfully had the original language of the Stevens proposal replaced by his own formulation, which contained the Constitution's current language about privileges or immunities, due process, and equal protection.

Much of the debate took place at a very abstract level. As one constitutional historian puts it, the framers of the Amendment "strove to have 'the truth . . . go out from every deliberative body in the land, as the rays of light radiate from the sun,'" and the framers "paid attention mainly to the substance of the great issues of principle to which they hoped to convert the nation, rather than to how their legal handiwork would be enforced in the future."[11] These grand aspirations did not prompt much careful analysis of the legalistic dimensions of the Amendment.

Nevertheless, there were some important comments on the first section of the Amendment, particularly the Privileges or Immunities Clause. Bingham explained that the effect of the Amendment was "to protect by national law . . . the inborn rights of every person within its jurisdiction whenever the same shall be abridged or denied by the unconstitutional acts of any State." In introducing the Fourteenth Amendment in the Senate, Senator Jacob Howard of

Michigan emphasized the Privileges or Immunities Clause and explicitly tied this clause to Bushrod Washington's sweeping language about fundamental rights in the *Corfield* case. He also made it clear that the courts were not yet finished with defining the contours of these rights. Rather, this was a work-in-progress. As with the P and I Clause in the original constitution, "questions arising under the clause [would] be discussed and adjudicated when they could happen practically to arise."

Modern scholars are often frustrated that the debates contain so little detail about the meaning of "privileges or immunities" or other terms such as "due process" and "equal protection." But no detailed explanation was needed. Everyone knew what these clauses were designed to accomplish. The Fourteenth Amendment followed on the heels of extensive debates about fundamental rights, their status under the law of nations, and their constitutional standing. As politicians, the Amendment's supporters could not entirely resist the opportunity to repeat what they all knew and had already said at length. Basically, however, they had thrashed over all of the issues before, and they knew what they meant when they referred to the "privileges and immunities" of American citizens: they meant the fundamental rights that had been proclaimed as an American birthright since the Declaration of Independence.

This view of the Fourteenth Amendment is, in the end, the one that fits most naturally with the constitutional text itself. In what may have been the single most influential book on constitutional law of the last thirty years, the late John Hart Ely made this point about as clearly as possible: the "most plausible interpretation of the Privileges or Immunities Clause is, as it must be, the one suggested by its language—that it was a delegation to future constitutional decision-makers to protect certain rights that the document neither lists, at least not exhaustively, nor even in any specific way gives directions for finding."[12]

Bingham's thinking (and that of other antislavery Republicans) was strikingly similar to the theories behind the Ninth Amendment. In both eras leading figures believed in "inborn" or "inalienable" rights, they agreed that these rights needed to be addressed in the Constitution, and they adopted broad constitutional language to prevent invasions of those rights. The Ninth Amendment protected fundamental rights from the federal government; the P or I Clause of the Fourteenth Amendment protected the same rights from state governments.

Some conservatives may consider all of this just "pie in the sky," suitable for political debate but lacking in legal significance. The people who wrote our Constitution disagreed.

PART TWO

Protecting Fundamental Rights

8

Fundamental Rights and the Due Process Clause

Since the Civil War era, the Supreme Court has indeed become a guardian of fundamental rights. However, the path that the Court took was circuitous. In the end, the Court did fulfill much of the Constitution's promise for human liberty, but it has never quite managed to find the right basis in the Constitution for doing so. Despite this confusion about where to base fundamental rights in the Constitution, judges have been able to articulate the nature of those rights with some success. Nevertheless, the shakiness of the textual basis for their decisions continues to raise doubts. They would be on much more solid ground if they relied on the Ninth Amendment and the P or I Clause of the Fourteenth Amendment.

THE SUBMERGENCE OF THE PRIVILEGES OR IMMUNITIES CLAUSE

Just as the Ninth Amendment was overlooked or misunderstood soon after its enactment, the P or I Clause itself pretty much disappeared from view within a decade of its enactment. The fatal blow was dealt when *The Slaughter House Cases*[1] were decided in 1873. You might be wondering what slaughterhouses have to do with fundamental rights. Through one of the accidents of history, a commonplace dispute over slaughterhouse regulations became the Court's first opportunity to explain the newly enacted Fourteenth Amendment.

The occasion for the Court's decision was a Louisiana law that banned slaughterhouses within the New Orleans city limits. The law made an exception for the Crescent City Company, which was essentially given a monopoly. The Supreme Court rejected a broad-gauged attack on the statute brought by New Orleans butchers. Examining each clause of the Fourteenth Amendment, the Court read them all very narrowly.

One of the butchers' arguments was based on the P or I Clause of the Fourteenth Amendment, which they claimed guaranteed their fundamental right to work at their trade. The Court held, however, that this clause protected only a limited set of national privileges like the right of access to federal authorities and the right to use navigable waters.

The Court held that privileges or immunities "of the United States" (protected by the Fourteenth Amendment) were limited to those that involved the citizen's relationship with the federal government. In contrast, the P and I Clause of the 1789 Constitution protected *state* privileges and immunities (but only in cases where a state discriminated against out-of-staters). Fundamental rights were solely part of state citizenship, the Court held, not federal citizenship. In so holding, the Court completely overlooked the fact that the P or I Clause in the Fourteenth Amendment had been modeled on the earlier clause and that key members of Congress referred to Justice Washington's fundamental rights ruling to explain their vision of the new provision. In effect, the Court gutted the Fourteenth Amendment's P or I Clause.

The four dissenters argued in vain that the Fourteenth Amendment clause was intended to protect the same fundamental rights as the earlier P and I Clause. The majority opinion is hard to justify. The legislative history showed quite clearly that Congress had something much broader in mind. Indeed, it is hard to see any reason for including the clause at all, if it meant as little as the Court suggested. All the rights covered by the clause under the Court's interpretation seemed to be rights that already flowed out of some other portions of federal law, making the clause redundant.

The bare five-Justice majority also ignored the changed meaning of state citizenship created by another portion of the Fourteenth Amendment. In order to ensure that slaves would be citizens, the first sentence of the Fourteenth Amendment conveyed federal and *state* citizenship on everyone born here. So now, state citizenship itself is a "privilege" that comes along with federal citizenship, which makes it hard to distinguish between the privileges and immunities of one and those of the other.

The majority also read other portions of the Fourteenth Amendment, such as due process and equal protection, as being extremely narrow. Those interpretations have not held up in later cases. But the Court's brutal assault on the P or I Clause was more successful.

With the disappearance of the Privileges or Immunities Clause from view (and the continuing amnesia about the Ninth Amendment), it was not clear whether the Constitution would provide any protection at all for fundamental rights. About fifteen years later, however, the Court found another constitutional site for fundamental rights: the Due Process Clause.

HOW FUNDAMENTAL RIGHTS CAME UNDER THE DUE PROCESS CLAUSE

It has now been more than two centuries since the Ninth Amendment was adopted, and much more than a century since the Fourteenth

Amendment went into effect. Either the Ninth Amendment or the P or I Clause of the Fourteenth Amendment could (and should) have provided a constitutional home for fundamental rights. But through an accident of history, the Supreme Court settled instead on another provision of the Fourteenth Amendment, the Due Process Clause. Despite occasional protests that this clause provides only procedural protections such as the right to a jury trial, the Court has insisted since the late nineteenth century that the Due Process Clause's guarantee of "liberty" encompasses substantive rights.

The Due Process Clause says only that the government cannot deprive a person of life, liberty, or property without due process of law. This sounds like it only requires some kind of legal proceeding such as a trial, but by 1887 the Court had fastened on a broader view of the clause. Under this view, the clause also protected certain fundamental rights from violation by state governments, regardless of what kinds of procedures the state used.

Picking the Due Process Clause as the home for fundamental rights was something of a historical accident, but not *completely* ungrounded. Before the Civil War, due process clauses in state constitutions were given varying interpretations by state courts. Many state courts rejected the theory that the Due Process Clause goes beyond fair procedures by allowing courts to review the substance of legislative policy decisions. On the other hand, an influential New York decision went the other way. And the 1860 Republican platform adopted the view that the Due Process Clause prohibited Congress from imposing slavery in the territories.

This view of due process, which obviously went beyond the merely procedural, was strongly endorsed by Bingham. Having imported at least some substantive content into due process, the supporters of the Fourteenth Amendment might have been willing to find protection for other fundamental rights in the same place. But compared to the wealth of evidence about the meaning of the P or I Clause, the historical evidence about fundamental rights and the Due Process Clause is relatively sparse. The P or I Clause and the Ninth Amendment would have given a much stronger basis for protecting fundamental rights from state governments. The Court's misstep has needlessly exposed it to much criticism.

Evolving Judicial Interpretations of Due Process

Initially, the Supreme Court primarily used the Due Process Clause to protect businesses from economic regulation. By using this doctrine to advance its own ideological agenda, the Court came close to bringing the whole idea of fundamental constitutional rights into dispute.

The most notorious case was *Lochner v. New York*, a case decided almost exactly a century ago.[2] In *Lochner*, the Court struck down a law protecting bakers from working excessive hours. New York prohibited employers from requiring bakers to work more than sixty hours a week. The Court viewed this as a violation of the fundamental right of bakers to work as many hours as they pleased. The majority proclaimed that the "general right to make a contract in relation to his business is part of the liberty of the individual protected by the Fourteenth Amendment." The Court could find no sufficient justification for restricting that individual liberty: people were entitled to work as many hours as they wanted without interference from the government. The decision has become a paradigm for judicial overreaching.

Even during this period, however, the Court had sometimes used the substantive due process doctrine to protect noneconomic rights. There is no constitutional provision that explicitly requires states to protect free speech. By its own terms, the First Amendment applies only to Congress. It seems clear that Congress thought it was achieving this goal through the P or I Clause, but that clause had long been forgotten by the time the issue arose. So the Court used the Due Process Clause as the vehicle for preventing state violations of freedom of speech, on the theory that free speech was a fundamental right. Ultimately, this theory would result in the "incorporation" of almost all of the Bill of Rights into the Due Process Clause.

The Court did not limit itself to protecting the enumerated rights that already applied to the federal government. The turning point came in a 1923 case. There, the Court declared unconstitutional a Nebraska law that prohibited teaching children in any language other than English. Two years later, the Court ruled that the state could not require all children to attend public schools. The Due Process Clause barred the state from using compulsory education laws to suppress private, especially religious, schools. These decisions provided the basis for modern-day rulings protecting privacy and family relationships.

In the Nebraska case, the Supreme Court emphasized that "the individual has certain fundamental rights which must be respected."[3] That was no proclamation by activist liberals—it came from a conservative court during Warren Harding's presidency. Modern-day conservatives may view this decision as activist. Judge Bork specifically listed it as one of the Court's decisions that would have to drop by the wayside under his view of constitutional law. The attacks on this case exemplify the degree to which today's conservative activists are seeking to overturn long-established precedents.

The 1920s cases established that the Due Process Clause also protected certain fundamental individual rights, quite apart from its controversial application to economic liberty. The Court made an important effort to articulate the meaning of fundamental rights, just at the time it was abandoning use of the Due Process Clause as restriction on economic regulation. Justice Benjamin Cardozo said that the test for whether a right was constitutionally protected was whether it was essential to ordered liberty. To be protected, he explained, a right must be so basic that abolishing it would violate a "principle of justice so rooted in the traditions and conscience of our people as to be ranked as fundamental."

An important step in protecting fundamental rights came during World War II, when the Court invalidated forced sterilization in a 1942 case involving a man convicted of stealing chickens. No doubt, the example of Nazi eugenics was on the Court's mind when it addressed the issue. The case involved an Oklahoma law that authorized sterilization of criminals with two or more felony convictions. (That was truly "three strikes and you're out" with a vengeance.) The opinion focused on the unequal treatment of the law, which had exemptions for various white-collar crimes such as embezzlement.

Of critical importance was the test that the Court articulated in the sterilization case. The Court held that the law required a compelling justification because it involved "one of the basic civil rights of man" and a "basic liberty." Thus, despite the Court's newfound deference to state legislation, it remained willing to provide at least a degree of protection to some unenumerated rights.

At the time, this must have seemed like a side issue. The big dispute was over the enumerated rights in the Bill of Rights and whether they were protected from state governments. Until the mid-1960s, the most heavily debated issue about Fourteenth Amendment due process was whether it protected provisions of the Bill of Rights such as the right against self-incrimination or double jeopardy. One by one, this and the other elements of the Bill of Rights were slowly incorporated into the Due Process Clause. Today, virtually the entire Bill of Rights has been incorporated into the Due Process Clause of the Fourteenth Amendment. The only clear exception is the right to jury trial in civil cases, though there is still some debate about the Second Amendment right to bear arms and the Eighth Amendment prohibition on excessive fines. We have ended up with something close to total application of the Bill of Rights to protect individuals from state government. This is one of the reasons that most people don't even know that the Bill of Rights itself applies only to the federal government, since the same rights are now recognized under the Fourteenth Amendment protections against state governments.

FUNDAMENTAL RIGHTS AND DUE PROCESS PROTECTION OF LIBERTY

Once this process incorporating enumerated rights was complete, the question was whether the Due Process Clause protected any other rights that might be essential to ordered liberty but not explicitly listed in the Bill of Rights. In the legal jargon of the time, the question was whether to go from total incorporation to total incorporation "plus." Did the Due Process Clause only protect the enumerated rights, or did it go further?

In the end, the prevailing view has been that due process covers more than fair procedures and the Bill of Rights. The classic explanation of this doctrine was given by Justice John Harlan in a predecessor to the 1965 *Griswold* ruling on contraceptives. Harlan was the great conservative dissenter from many of the Warren Court's most controversial decisions like *Miranda*. He was a harsh critic of judicial activism, but he did believe that courts had a responsibility to protect fundamental rights.

Justice Harlan maintained that "full scope of the liberty guaranteed by the Due Process Clause cannot be found in or limited by the precise terms of the specific guarantees elsewhere provided in the Constitution." According to Harlan, liberty "is not a series of isolated points pricked out in terms of the taking of property; the freedom of speech, press, and religion; the right to keep and bear arms; the freedom from unreasonable searches and seizures; and so on." Rather, constitutional liberty is "a rational continuum which, broadly speaking, includes a freedom from all substantial arbitrary impositions and purposeless restraints," as well as a requirement for special justification when certain critical interests are invaded by the state.

Harlan's theory of the meaning of constitutional liberty proved to have a great influence on Rehnquist Court Justices such as Kennedy, Souter, and O'Connor. It helped provide much of the basis for their decision to reaffirm the core of *Roe v. Wade*, rather than overruling it, as many had predicted would happen at the time.

Justice Harlan also had something to say about the nature of fundamental rights. He explained that due process "has not been reduced to any formula; its content cannot be determined by reference to any code. The best that can be said is that through this Court's decisions it has represented the balance which our Nation, built upon postulates of respect for the liberty of the individual, has struck between that liberty and the demands of organized society." In striking this balance, Harlan explained, the Court must look at the country's living tradition. A decision "which radically departs from it [the living tradition] could not long survive, while a decision which builds on what has survived is likely to be sound." "No formula," he said, "could serve as a substitute, in this area, for judgment and restraint."

Several things about Justice Harlan's formulation set him apart from modern conservatives like Justice Scalia. Scalia thinks that law should consist only of sharp, clearly defined rules. Harlan realized that liberty is too expansive a concept to be reduced to a formula. Scalia also likes to talk about American traditions, but his idea of a tradition is something that has stayed static and unchanged for decades or centuries. In contrast, Harlan spoke of the living traditions of the American people, recognizing that traditions grow and change, and that the same basic principles may appear in very different guises at different times.

Justice Harlan was right in his constitutional vision of liberty, but he attached it to the wrong part of the Constitution. The Ninth Amendment was written to express precisely his vision of liberty as transcending the few "pinpricks" in the Bill of Rights. That vision was brought to bear on the states by the P or I Clause of the Fourteenth Amendment. But lawyers are by nature prone to follow the well-beaten path of precedent, and by Harlan's time, these concepts had become linked with the idea of due process. Although a few Justices now and then have referred back to the true source, the Ninth Amendment, the Court has stuck to due process, making its decisions more vulnerable to attack.

The Court has also failed to take advantage of the possible support for its decisions offered by the P or I Clause. Today, this clause remains almost forgotten. The only exception was a brief reappearance in 1999. In *Saenz v. Roe*,[4] the Court used the clause to strike down a state law limiting the welfare benefits of new residents. For the first twelve months of residence in the state, new arrivals were limited to the amount of welfare payments they would have received in their home state. The Court held that the right to move to a state and be treated as equal to all other residents was a privilege or immunity protected by the Fourteenth Amendment. Notably, a dissent by Justice Thomas recounted historical evidence suggesting that the clause was meant to protect an array of fundamental rights. Also notably, Justice Scalia did not join the dissent. Both Scalia and Thomas are on the right wing of the Court, but Thomas is more of a libertarian, while Scalia's sympathies seem to be with social conservatives. Perhaps *Saenz* will prove to be a first step in reviving the P or I Clause, but it is too soon to tell.

With the exception of this recent case, the P or I Clause remains almost forgotten, just like the Ninth Amendment. Given that the Court did much the same thing through the Due Process Clause, the confusion may not have actually affected the outcomes of many cases. But using the Due Process Clause has made the Court more vulnerable to attack. The P or I Clause by its very terms protects an individual's substantive rights, while the Due Process Clause looks more like a guarantee of fair trials. The historical basis for using the Due Process Clause to protect fundamental rights is much weaker. As a result, the Court has opened the door to attacks on the whole enterprise of using fundamental rights by using the wrong clause.

Those attacks ought to be rejected. The Court may be using the wrong clause, but it is doing just what the creators of the Ninth and Fourteenth Amendments envisioned when it protects fundamental rights. Recognizing the central role of the Ninth Amendment and the P or I Clause would go a long way toward eliminating any doubt about the historical basis for the Court's rulings and rebutting critics who consider the modern rulings to be illegitimate.

9

Fundamental Rights Today

Justice Harlan's views about the meaning of liberty remain influential today. In 1992, when the Court reaffirmed the 1973 *Roe v. Wade* abortion ruling, the opinion quoted Justice Harlan at length. Following Harlan's lead, the opinion stressed the "premise of the Constitution that there is a realm of personal liberty which the government may not enter." Most Americans seem to agree with that general proposition—Bork's contrary view was one reason why his nomination to the Supreme Court foundered. But the harder question is how to give concrete content to this vision of liberty.

To my mind, the real problem is not the existence of fundamental rights but their definition. History leaves little room for doubt that the fundamental rights are protected. Even without knowing the history, the simple language of the Ninth Amendment and the Fourteenth Amendment, if read carefully and taken seriously, establishes the same point. I suspect that even many opponents of fundamental rights doctrine secretly understand this. What brings them up short is the line-drawing problem. How do we determine whether a right counts as fundamental? How can judges make this determination without simply imposing their own moral and political viewpoint on the rest of us? Are there any objective guidelines?

I will discuss my own answers to these questions in a later chapter. It is only fair, however, to begin by examining how the Supreme Court has tackled these issues.

WHAT RIGHTS HAS THE COURT PROTECTED?

The first half of this book has been dedicated to proving that the idea of fundamental rights rests on solid historical bedrock. The task ahead is to begin to define those rights. In thinking about the definition of fundamental rights, it is helpful to briefly review the Court's rulings on the subject. Examining these cases also helps show what is at stake in the modern debate, for the benefit of any readers who might wonder about the real-life impact of the theoretical issues I am discussing.

One cluster of Supreme Court cases involves reproductive rights. In the World War II era, as we have seen, the Court rejected forced sterilization. It said that the case involved "one of the basic civil rights of man," a right "fundamental to the very existence and survival of the race."[1] Twenty years later, the Court followed up in *Griswold* with the right of a married couple to use contraception, a right it soon extended to the unmarried. Next of course, was the abortion ruling. These cases will be discussed in detail in a later chapter, as well as the Court's rulings on the right to die. There is also a cluster of cases protecting family relationships. These cases provide a good sense of how the Court views fundamental rights. They also show just what is at stake in the dispute over fundamental rights, and they highlight the ongoing debate over the legitimacy of those rights.

In the 1977 *Moore* case, for example, an Ohio city zoning ordinance defined a "single family" dwelling so narrowly that it was illegal for a grandmother to raise a grandchild in her home.[2] She already had one son and his child living in the home, but this was allowed under the zoning ordinance in a special exception. Adding the second child broke the law.

It is worth repeating the language, reminiscent of a tax code, by which the city defined the limits of acceptable family living: "Notwithstanding the provisions of subsection (b) hereof, a family may include not more than one dependent married or unmarried child of the nominal head of the household or of the spouse of the nominal head of the household and the spouse and dependent children of such dependent child." Notice that this exemption applies only if all the grandchildren have the same parent. It is okay for two brothers to live with their grandmother, but not two first cousins. So when a second grandchild moved in with Grandma Moore after his mother's death, he did not qualify since he was a first cousin rather than a sibling. To reward grandma for taking in this motherless child, the city sentenced her to five days in jail.

Is this really America that we're talking about here? Apparently so. In fact, four Justices voted to uphold the conviction. They thought that the city had engaged in a reasonable exercise of its zoning power, simply engaging in routine line drawing in its definition of family.

Fortunately, the majority thought otherwise. Justice Lewis Powell, the great centrist judge of the Burger Court era, wrote the lead opinion. He said that "when the government intrudes on choices concerning family living arrangements, this Court must examine carefully the importance of the governmental interests advanced and the extent to which they are served by the challenged regulation." He pointed out the utter arbitrariness of the zoning ordinance: "The ordinance would permit a grandmother to live with a single dependent son and children, even if his school-age children number a dozen, yet it forces Mrs. Moore to find another dwelling for her grandson John, simply because of the presence of his uncle and cousin in the same household."

Since the *Moore* ruling, most of the Court has agreed that family-related rights are fundamental. However, some judges have emphatically rejected the Supreme Court's endorsement of "family values." The ongoing dispute on this score is exemplified by the *Troxel* case, another situation involving the family rights of grandparents.[3]

Like many family law cases, the facts had the making of a TV miniseries. Tommie Granville and her boyfriend, Brad Troxel, had a relationship that ended in 1991. They never married, but they had two daughters. After the couple separated, Brad moved back in with his parents and often brought the girls home for weekend visits. Brad committed suicide in 1993, but the grandparents continued to see the girls on a regular basis after their son's death. After a couple of years, however, Tommie decided to limit them to one short visit per month. The grandparents went to court under a Washington State law that authorizes any person (relative or not) to file suit for visitation rights.

The Supreme Court agreed that the statute was unconstitutional, but there was some disagreement about the specific flaw in the statute. Justice O'Connor wrote an opinion for herself and three other judges; two other Justices found somewhat different flaws in the statute. There was general agreement, however, with Justice O'Connor's premise that the "liberty interest at issue in this case—the interest of parents in the care, custody, and control of their children—is perhaps the oldest of the fundamental liberty interests recognized by this Court." She traced this right back to the 1920s cases that condemned restrictions on parental control over the education of their children.

CURRENT APPROACHES TO DEFINING FUNDAMENTAL RIGHTS

Even judges who agree on the general principle of protecting unenumerated rights have not always been able to agree on just which rights are protected. In the next chapters, I will examine some of the specific questions that have divided them. By considering the question in the context of developing U.S. and international legal norms, it is actually possible to answer most of these questions fairly confidently—even in such tough cases as assisted suicide and gay marriage. That old idea of the Framers—the "law of nations"— remains an enlightening guideline even today.

This brings us back to Kennedy's opinion in *Lawrence* (the sodomy case). His efforts to define liberty were useful, though he would have done better to rely on the Ninth Amendment. In Justice Kennedy's opinion, we can see the outlines of a workable test for determining whether a right is fundamental.

In defending the proposition that liberty includes the right to engage in same-sex relationships, Kennedy relied on a variety of sources:

- The general thrust of the Supreme Court's jurisprudence on privacy issues, which tended to reject interference with intimate relationships (even though the Court had previously upheld a sodomy ban in an aberrational decision)
- State court decisions holding sodomy laws unconstitutional under their own state constitutions
- A strong trend toward abolition of sodomy laws by state legislatures
- Decisions of international human rights tribunals, particularly in Europe, that had rejected sodomy bans

Justice Kennedy's eclectic approach to constitutional interpretation shocked Justice Scalia, not to mention the even more irate social conservatives in Congress. But it was Kennedy, rather than these conservatives, who was most true to the vision of James Madison and his generation. Looking at this broad array of sources makes perfect sense from the Framers' law of nations perspective. After all, Framers like John Adams believed "that a lawyer ought never to be without a volume of natural or public law, or moral philosophy, on his table or in his pocket."

The international law of human rights is the modern counterpart of what earlier generations called "the law of nations." If we wish to be true to the Framers and their constitutional legacy, we should, like them, turn to international law as one source of guidance. Of course many conservatives regard this as a terrible idea. But for originalists, whether we think this is a good idea is supposed to be irrelevant. If looking beyond our own borders for legal guidance is a terrible idea, blame the Framers!

I will return to this question later in the book because this controversy calls for a more extended discussion. The bottom line, however, is that what Justice Kennedy did in the sodomy case is completely consistent with the views of the Framers and with a long history of reliance on foreign law by the Supreme Court. Justice Scalia was simply wrong to view this practice as a radical innovation or as somehow anti-American.

In considering the sodomy decision and other recent rulings, it is also important to realize that the fundamental rights doctrine itself is equally well-founded. The vision that lies behind the Ninth Amendment (and its successor, the Fourteenth Amendment's Privileges or Immunities Clause) mandates that our government respect our basic rights as human beings. The Ninth Amendment tells us that basic rights are not a gift to the American people from legal documents like the Bill of Rights. Instead, these rights existed before the Constitution was even adopted. In enforcing these rights in its decisions, the modern Supreme Court is merely being true to the Framers' vision. And in turn, the Framers were following an even older tradition of belief in natural rights.

It seems a little late in the day to reject the idea of fundamental rights. There are now eight decades of precedent on fundamental rights. Still, is it possible to provide reasonable guidelines on how to identify them? The only way to answer this question is to address some of the most controversial issues that the Court has encountered, so we can see if there is a firm basis for determining which rights are fundamental.

10

An Invitation to Activism?

The first order of business, actually, is to establish that some things do *not* qualify as unenumerated rights. We need to do this in order to combat the fear that enforcing the Ninth Amendment would leave courts free to enforce any and all "rights" that might strike their fancy. In short, we do not need to be afraid that resurrecting the Ninth Amendment will lead to a revival of the *Lochner*-era sin of using the fundamental rights doctrine as a screen for political ideology.

Fear of unwarranted judicial intrusion on democratic decisions is the biggest barrier to accepting the teaching of the Ninth Amendment. It seems clear that the Constitution recognizes the existence of fundamental, unenumerated rights. The more troublesome question is whether courts should enforce fundamental rights against the actions of other governmental bodies. Two important arguments have been made against judicial enforcement: it is subject to abuse, and it always involves some sacrifice of our strong belief in majority rule. Even when we do something that seems as sensible as protecting the right of a grandmother to take care of her grandson, we are limiting the right of local elected officials, responsive to the city's majority views, to enact the legislation of their choice. And of course, we cannot be sure that all judicial rulings will involve such clear-cut abuses of government power as the grandmother case.

These are powerful arguments for caution, but they do not support complete judicial withdrawal. As the Federalists said in the debates on the Constitution, any power can be abused, but this fear in itself cannot be sufficient to justify eliminating a governmental power. As to what is called the "countermajoritarian difficulty," this is always a concern, but sometimes more so than others. Sometimes, the Court may not actually be opposing the view of a majority of the population. For example, in enforcing a fundamental right, the Court may be intervening to correct a breakdown in the normal process of representation, or the decision in question may be an aberration issuing from some eccentric local government and contrary to clear national consensus.

Moreover, although majority rule is obviously a very good thing, it is a mistake to transform this observation into an absolute. Sometimes slavish adherence to the norm of majority rule may involve unacceptable sacrifices of other critically important values. Do we really have to prove our belief in democracy by sending Grandma Moore to jail for trying to take care of her motherless grandson? Unless we place an *infinite* value on majority rule, there must be *some* situations in which a small intrusion on this value is justified to avoid a major loss of some other value.

The remaining argument against legal recognition of fundamental rights is that there simply is no way a court can distinguish a fundamental right from any other personal interest. In its strong form (that there is no way at all to distinguish fundamental rights from any other personal interest), this argument is untenable. As a society we do share some notions about the relative importance of various personal interests. Few people seriously think, for example, that the right to eat popcorn is as important as the right to raise one's own children. Almost everyone would agree that a law that indis-

criminately removed children from their homes violates a fundamental right. At some level, then, can't we all agree that certain government actions violate fundamental rights?

A critic of fundamental rights might respond with a more nu-
anced argument. True, the critic might say, some government actions would be universally condemned. But in a democracy those
kinds of abominations are unlikely. In reality the kinds of issues that
actually end up in court will all be in the gray area where reasonable
people (maybe even a majority) think the government is acting le-
gitimately. Courts will encounter few black-and-white cases. In
those instances when a majority has actually chosen to invade an arguably fundamental right, it may be too difficult for courts to make
a principled determination whether the right should be considered
fundamental. More likely, judges will simply resort to their personal
values to decide these cases. So isn't judicial enforcement of fundamental rights an invitation to activism?

No, not really. Rather than being an invitation to judicial activism, Justice Kennedy's approach actually restrains the Court by
making it part of a larger community of courts and lawmakers. Justices should not merely consider their own views but also take into
account the views of other federal and state judges, of legislators
throughout the country, and of judges and lawmakers around the
world. The Court will not necessarily follow any of these sources of
guidance unquestioningly, but it will not be left in the dark either.

One way to see the benefits of this approach is to contrast it with
what the Court did during what has been called the *Lochner* period.
(Recall that in the *Lochner* case itself, the Court struck down a sixty-
hour work week for bakers.) During this period, stretching from the
late nineteenth century to the middle of the New Deal, the
Supreme Court struck down legislation that it deemed to violate
freedom of contract. After the New Deal, this approach to constitutional law became infamous.

The *Lochner* Court might have prevented its errors if it had approached the question differently. There was little support for recognizing a human right to be free from labor regulation: the Court's previous decisions had not established a broad immunity from government regulation of contracts; the trend in state legislatures, Congress, and Europe was toward greater labor regulation, not less; and the state courts were at most mixed. Thus, it would have been hard to make a serious case for any emerging consensus of national or international authority in favor of unregulated labor relations. If the *Lochner* Court had followed the methods that Justice Kennedy later used, it would have realized that economic regulation does not violate human rights.

The *Lochner* Court might also have done well to consider the lessons of American history. The idea of natural economic rights is contrary to much of our tradition. Benjamin Franklin, for example, once said that "Private Property . . . is a Creature of Society, and is subject to the Calls of that Society, whenever its Necessities shall require it, even to its last Farthing; its contributions therefore to the public Exigencies are . . . to be considered . . . the Return of an obligation previously received, or the Payment of a just Debt." Franklin's views were typical of the colonial and revolutionary period. Even when individualism became more prominent in the period before the framing of the Constitution, it was not understood to entail absolute property rights. The "Taking Clause," for example, was narrowly understood to cover only the physical seizure of property by the government. (This clause requires compensation when the government takes private property for public use.)

One problem with *Lochner* is that it had no limits as a basis for judicial intervention into public policy. Almost everything human beings do that is worth regulating involves the combined action of at least two people (if not of enormous multinational corporations). Thus, complete freedom of contract really means complete freedom to do what you want, unless a judge happens to agree that a specific regulation is reasonable. Taking *Lochner* seriously would give judges an unlimited warrant to review legislation of all kinds, in effect transferring the legislative power from Congress to the judges. Recognizing a carefully delimited sphere of fundamental rights is different. It neither requires a widespread restructuring of existing governmental operations nor places the Court in the position of routinely determining the reasonableness of all legislation. The right to freedom of contract and relating interests in economic autonomy is simply much broader than the more limited rights protected by the Ninth Amendment.

Interpreting the Ninth Amendment as an open-ended guarantee of "property rights" would be equally ill-advised. The Constitution does require compensation when the government seizes property, and the Supreme Court has interpreted that guarantee to apply when a government regulation amounts to a seizure in everything but name. But the Court has also properly recognized that the attributes of property ownership are defined by state law. The federal Constitution does not contain a federal code of property law governing each of the fifty states. Each state has its own rules of property law, and those rules have evolved over time. There are libertarian authors who believe that philosophical theory or economics can provide definitive answers about the ownership and control of property. But they have never succeeded in finding a legal foundation for their position, as opposed to their own personal visions of justice.

Still, even if the list of fundamental rights is limited at any one time, perhaps courts would be free to create new constitutional rights on demand, making the Ninth Amendment just as dangerous as *Lochner* in the long run. Inch by inch, the Court might take on new territory. If the Court is free to declare new constitutional rights at will, the scope of its power may be effectively unlimited.

This argument probably gained force from the Supreme Court's abortion decision, *Roe v. Wade*, in which the Court seemed quite blithe about identifying a new fundamental right. In explaining why abortion was a fundamental right, the Court was too cursory, as if it found implying such rights an easy matter requiring little justification. Because Justice Blackmun was fairly offhand in that opinion when he explained why abortion is a fundamental right, a similarly offhand argument might suffice to create additional fundamental rights. Thus, *Roe* would become the first step down a slippery slope, with new fundamental rights being created willy-nilly. Or so critics of fundamental rights might argue. But this argument has proved unfounded. The Court has not enthusiastically created new fundamental rights on the basis of the *Roe* model. Instead, it has proceeded cautiously, often rejecting calls to recognize sweeping new rights or deferring any intervention until the political process has had time to address an issue. As we have seen, the Court has by and large stuck with a few well-defined areas relating to family life. So long as we refrain from appointing wild-eyed idealists to the Court, we do not need to fear that reliance on the Ninth Amendment will open the floodgates to an unending succession of new fundamental rights.

In *Lawrence* (the Texas case), Justice Scalia argued that having struck down sodomy laws, the Court would be committed to striking down laws against bestiality or public masturbation. This is a wild, misguided charge. Where is the groundswell of support, in the states or internationally, for considering bestiality and public masturbation to be fundamental human rights? An opinion trying to make such a claim would not get off the ground. Where we do see a broad consensus, however, is for the right to use contraceptives, to have abortions under at least some circumstances, and to refuse medical treatment in order to die with dignity. It is these rights that movement conservatives find so anathema, but only because these critics themselves are out of the national and interna-

tional mainstream. Indeed, it is Justice Kennedy and not Justice
Scalia, despite all his bravado, whose constitutional vision is faithful
to the Framers.

The previous chapters have laid the groundwork for understanding how the concept of fundamental rights, rooted in the Ninth
Amendment, has a legitimate home in constitutional law. It's time
to pull the pieces together by showing how the Ninth Amendment
can actually be applied. After first discussing some general issues in
defining fundamental rights, I will turn to concrete examples such
as abortion and assisted suicide.

11

A User's Guide to the Ninth Amendment

As we have seen, the Ninth Amendment and its cousin, the Privileges or Immunities Clause of the Fourteenth Amendment, establish the existence of fundamental, unenumerated rights. Those rights can be applied by courts to overturn oppressive laws, but they have other uses beyond this kind of judicial review. Whatever use we make of the idea of fundamental rights, we have to determine which rights are fundamental and which are not. After considering some of the potential applications of the idea of fundamental rights, I will turn to the question of how to define them.

BEYOND JUDICIAL REVIEW

The most obvious use of the Ninth Amendment is to justify court decisions invalidating laws like the zoning ordinance that sent Grandma Moore to jail. Despite my best efforts, some readers may remain skeptical of that point. Partly for the benefit of those readers, it is important to explain how Ninth Amendment rights could have real legal significance even if courts do not use them as a basis for judicial review.

Apart from their potential as a basis for invalidating legislation, the Ninth Amendment and its Fourteenth Amendment cousin have two other important uses. First, they provide a basis for the creation of congressional legislation dealing with fundamental rights. Article I of the Constitution contains the Necessary and Proper Clause, which authorizes Congress to pass whatever legislation is necessary and proper to implement its own powers or those of the other branches of the federal government. Legislation designed to ensure that neither the courts nor the executive branch violates Ninth Amendment rights is unquestionably "necessary and proper" if Congress thinks that there is some risk of constitutional violations. Even if courts were to be found to lack the ability to enforce the Ninth Amendment *against* Congress, it could at least serve as a basis for action *by* Congress to prevent the executive branch from violating fundamental rights. Given some of the extravagant claims for presidential power that have sometimes been made, it is important to be clear that Congress has the ability to check the president where fundamental rights are concerned.

Similarly, Congress can also enforce fundamental rights against the states.[1] Section 5 of the Fourteenth Amendment gives Congress the power to enforce the amendment's provisions, and the P or I Clause is one of those provisions. Hence, if Congress has sufficient grounds for concluding that states may invade fundamental rights protected by that clause, it is empowered to legislate in order to protect those rights. For example, Congress should have the power to legislate to prevent cities from passing zoning ordinances of the kind that ensnared Grandma Moore.

Another potential use for the Ninth Amendment is in terms of statutory interpretation. During the period when the Constitution was drafted, courts interpreted statutes quite freely when necessary in order to bring them into accord with natural rights, equity, and the law of nations. Similarly, today, courts should feel free to interpret statutes so as to further the aims of the Ninth Amendment. For example, statutes should not be construed to deviate from well-established principles of international human rights law, unless this interpretation is absolutely unavoidable.

Thus, even those who do not think that the Ninth Amendment justifies courts in striking down legislation should still be willing to countenance other ways of giving indirect effect to the Ninth Amendment, whether through congressional action to protect fundamental rights or through judicial interpretation of statutes to avoid infringing rights.

But there is no reason to settle for these half-measures. We should treat unenumerated fundamental rights as being on a par with the enumerated rights that courts enforce, rather than "disparaging" them by treating them as second-class rights. In short, Ninth Amendment rights deserve not only indirect protection by the courts but direct application.

Natural Rights for the Modern Lawyer

The Ninth Amendment makes it clear that unenumerated rights are valid, but just because those rights are not written down, that does not mean they are immune from the normal tools of the lawyer's craft. Rather, the Ninth Amendment calls on us to treat unenumerated rights like the enumerated ones—as the subject of ordinary legal analysis. To treat them as less "legal" than rights such as free speech would disparage them in just the way the Ninth Amendment forbids.

Applying the Constitution's fundamental rights guarantees does pose some special problems that are not posed by more specific constitutional provisions. There is no doubt that a court enforcing the

First Amendment may have to address thorny issues and that the answers are often controversial. But a court deciding a First Amendment case does have the assurance that the Constitution has something to say about the case. How to apply the First Amendment may be difficult, but at least no one doubts that the Constitution really does protect some forms of speech.

When we leave the specific provisions of the Bill of Rights, however, the very relevance of the Constitution becomes questionable. Before even addressing what the Constitution has to say about abortion, for example, we have to face doubts about whether it has anything to say about the matter. If the question had arisen, the Framers might have addressed it by looking at natural law, as articulated by philosophers like Locke and jurists like Vattel. Today, however, the vocabulary of natural law is less well accepted.

Natural law is not a popular theory among lawyers today. Many find it to be suspiciously moralistic and lacking in rigorous analysis. Natural law seems to leave the law floating above us in some stratospheric level of abstraction, rather than anchored in the world of constitutional text, statutes, and precedents. But to follow this approach, we do not have to believe that human rights have some metaphysical existence independent of our own perspectives and needs. What we must believe is that civilized people share an aspiration toward protecting human dignity and that we can learn from each other how to give concrete meaning to this aspiration. We can reason together even if we lack some transcendental ability to sense objective moral truths.

TRADITION, CONSENSUS, AND OTHER GUIDEPOSTS

A particularly important question is the role of American traditions in identifying fundamental rights. The Justices disagree about the correct methodology for interpreting tradition. One group of Justices believes that the asserted right needs to be "carefully" (and by implication, narrowly) defined, with the next step being a comparison with concrete examples of deeply rooted historical American rights. Others argue for a broader approach.

Justice David Souter has been the most articulate advocate of the broader position. He argues that the Court should not necessarily look for a long-standing national consensus about the very specific claim for constitutional protection. Demanding such specific historical endorsement would, he said, produce legal petrifaction; rather, it is important to "understand old principles afresh by new examples and counterexamples," shifting the boundaries of those principles over time.[2]

Interpreting traditions can be a tricky business. It would narrow the focus too much to demand that a very specific practice must have been in place since the American Revolution, unquestioned and without change. Such tradition is akin to a "living fossil," like the cockroach that has survived for a long time without change. Traditions normally evolve over time, and at any given time they may be subject to dispute. If we are too loose in our definition of tradition, however, history can give courts very little guidance.

The problem of exactly how to define tradition is hugely important if, as some judges seem to think, tradition is the sole determinant of what constitutes a fundamental right. It is less critical in the approach I am advocating. Tradition is only one element in the ultimate determination of whether something qualifies as a fundamental right. Traditions that are more concrete and have longer histories get more weight in the analysis. Broadly conceived traditions are also important, but they will not carry the day without more specific support from other elements of the test.

Traditions do not come neatly packaged in a way that provides clear answers to constitutional questions. But a judge should be able to show that a value has genuine roots in our traditions. The argument is even stronger if the judge can show that failure to apply a more traditional value in a particular context has been due to factors that do not deserve respect, such as racist or sexist prejudices or resentment of political dissenters.

Contemporary social consensus is another important factor. Obviously, the greater the consensus about a value, the more comfortable a judge can feel. This may seem like an irrelevancy for a constitutional court, since consensus is presumably reflected in legislation and therefore does not need constitutional protection. However, the truth is more complicated.

In reality, courts do sometimes find themselves confronting a law that deviates from a widespread consensus. First, on important issues, a national consensus may exist without being reflected in every region or locality. The most striking example was segregation, which was entrenched in the South but had little credibility at the national level. President Harry Truman had already desegregated the armed forces before the Court even considered the issue of segregation. Other examples are the ban on contraception in a handful of states in the 1960s and the criminalizing of homosexual acts in a few states in the 1990s. The question of how much localities should be allowed to deviate from a fundamental national consensus is not necessarily easy, but it should not give rise to grave concerns about the legitimacy of judicial action.

Second, it is naïve to assume that important value issues are always deliberated through the legislative process before law is made. Political actors have significant discretion, which they can use even in the face of a public consensus about values. Also, political expediency and weak resolve can cause politicians to avoid confronting issues in order to avoid offending narrow constituencies regardless of majority views. As recent history shows, important constitutional interests can be invaded without full debate through Executive fiat. A key role of the courts is to combat this risk by requiring that the

Executive return to Congress for clear authorization before step-ping into constitutionally dangerous territory. Even within Con-gress, constitutional issues can be suppressed, as when a rider is attached to critical legislation at the last minute. Constitutional liti-gation can help defend consensus values against such sneak attacks. Thus, a clear consensus may sometimes exist but not be reflected accurately by legislation. One important judicial task can be to pre-vent governmental officials from invading rights that are firmly em-bedded in a national consensus.

Courts will not always have the benefit of a clear consensus, how-ever. At the very least, judges should look for whether there is broad support for a value, even if not consensus—for example, whether support for the value cuts across party lines. It is also important to consider how lawmakers and other judges have approached a sub-ject. Although legislation can sometimes reflect a lack of delibera-tion or special interest influence, it often does provide a guide to the views of the public and of thoughtful public officials.

The same kinds of issues that face the Supreme Court are also en-countered by other judges. State judges may have the task of defin-ing fundamental rights under their own state constitutions. And foreign jurists may face very similar issues in interpreting interna-tional human rights agreements or their national constitutions. Their well-reasoned views are also entitled to consideration; we should not assume that we have a monopoly on wisdom in the United States.

Another key factor is precedent. Previous Supreme Court rulings may settle whether a particular right is fundamental. Precedents also provide a basis for reasoning by analogy. The more something resembles an already established fundamental right, the more likely it is to qualify as fundamental itself. A similar process of reasoning by analogy applies to the specific provisions of the Bill of Rights. The more closely connected a right is to the specific guarantees of the Bill of Rights, the more likely it is to be fundamental.

Putting all of this together, we have the following list of factors to be considered in determining whether a given right is fundamental:

- Supreme Court precedent establishing the right or analogous rights
- Connections with specific constitutional guarantees
- Long-standing, specific traditions upholding the right
- Contemporary societal consensus about the validity of the right
- Decisions by American lawmakers and judges recognizing the right
- Broader or more recent American traditions consistent with the right
- Decisions by international lawmakers and judges recognizing the right

These factors are not listed in any specific order, but in general, the items earlier on the list are likely to get more weight. The factors lower on the list become more relevant when the earlier factors are absent or ambiguous. But the ordering should not be considered too rigid. It would be a waste of time to agonize too much about the exact order of the list, when each case is likely to present its own special problems.

Does this approach actually work? The only way to find out is to try out the approach on some hard questions and see how well it functions.

PART THREE

Applying the Ninth Amendment

12

Reproductive Rights

It would take another book to work out fully the implications of this vision for current constitutional disputes. But we can easily see the implications for some of the major disputes of today. The Ninth Amendment not only strengthens the legitimacy of the Court's enforcement of unenumerated rights; with its linkage to the law of nations, it also provides guidance on how to define and apply these rights based on evolving national and international norms. The abortion issue provides what may be the toughest test for these concepts.

ASSESSING *ROE V. WADE*

The most fundamental question raised in the *Roe* case was whether the right to an abortion could be derived from earlier precedent or whether it was a complete invention by Justice Blackmun. Conceding that the Constitution does not contain an explicit right of privacy,[1] Blackmun relied on a series of rulings finding some aspect of privacy to be protected by the First, Fourth, Fifth, and Ninth Amendments, and by the concept of liberty in the Fourteenth Amendment. He viewed those cases as showing that privacy extends to aspects of "marriage, procreation, contraception, family relationships, and child rearing and education."[2] Justice Blackmun then argued that this right of family or reproductive privacy was broad enough to cover "a woman's decision whether or not to terminate her pregnancy."[3]

Justice Blackmun was correct to identify a cluster of cases protecting various aspects of privacy and a tighter cluster relating to intimate relations and reproductive choice. This makes his characterization of abortion as a constitutionally protected decision plausible on the basis of precedent. Still, the analysis of precedent seems strikingly incomplete. He clearly could have done more to explain how these cases relate to each other, and what they have to do with the Fourteenth Amendment's reference to liberty.

Despite the vehemence of the attacks on *Roe*, it seems clear that the Court was correct in classifying procreative rights as fundamental. Although these rights were not discussed specifically in connection with the Fourteenth Amendment, historians suggest that Civil War–era Republicans, who drafted and enacted the amendment, considered rights relating to the family fundamental. American society has traditionally drawn a distinction between public matters involving government and the marketplace and private matters involving the family.

Furthermore, as Justice Blackmun observed, a line of Supreme Court decisions going back many years had granted parenthood and procreation a fundamental constitutional status. We have already seen how the Court previously protected the right to use contraception and the right to be free from compulsory sterilization. Thus, procreation was well within the ambit of precedent. That the Court was not simply imaginatively rewriting precedent is indicated by the number of lower court judges who had correctly anticipated *Roe* on the basis of similar reasoning. Popular consensus also supported the *Roe* Court's recognition of at least a limited right to an abortion, with a large majority of the public favoring legalization of abortion under at least some circumstances.

Given the presence of a fundamental right, the Court was obligated to assess independently a state's justification for infringing on the right. What makes *Roe* so difficult is the strength of the countervailing interest asserted by the state: the interest in preserving human life. Few issues in contemporary law or politics are more controversial or deeply emotional than the validity of this justification. *Roe* is a hard case in more ways than one. Nevertheless, my view is that the Court was correct in holding a total ban on abortion unconstitutional.

In particular, I doubt that the interest in preserving human life is sufficiently implicated to justify banning all abortions before the eighth week of pregnancy—a category that includes most abortions. Spontaneous abortions are quite common in early pregnancy, so any given embryo may or may not make it to the end of pregnancy. Before the twelfth week, the fetus does not engage in organized movement. At twelve weeks, its brain weighs only about ten grams (about the weight of two quarters). The cerebral cortex (the main distinction between humans and animals) is primitive and tiny. Brain wave studies also suggest that consciousness probably cannot begin any earlier than the twelfth week at the earliest. These facts make it difficult to say that the fetus has already become in any real sense a living person. The possibility that it will later become a person gives the fetus moral value, but this possibility is itself conditioned on the woman's willingness to continue the pregnancy, the very question at issue. Against this value must be weighed the powerful reasons that may impel a woman to choose an abortion. On balance, preservation of the fetus, at a point in pregnancy when consciousness could not yet exist, is too weak a justification to eliminate completely the woman's fundamental interest in deciding whether to bear a child.

If only my personal assessment of the status of abortion were involved, I would be troubled about making it the basis for a constitutional holding on such a difficult question. In reality, however, this assessment is not merely personal. In particular, the public's support for embryonic stem cell research indicates that most people do not consider early embryos to be full-fledged persons.

Moreover, most Americans believe that abortion is permissible to preserve the mother's health or to prevent the birth of a deformed child. There is an equally widespread belief that a woman pregnant as the result of rape or incest is entitled to an abortion. Logically, these views are inconsistent with a claim that fetuses are entitled to be treated as persons legally. None of these circumstances would be considered sufficient justification for murder, so the implicit assumption must be that less than the death of an actual person is at stake. This societal consensus is inconsistent with a belief that preservation of the fetus automatically outweighs the woman's vital interests.

Thus, in seeking to impose a complete ban on abortion, the state is invading a fundamental right based on a justification that the great majority of Americans, for good reason, do not accept. Given this social consensus, a court would be well justified in rejecting the "right to life" justification and hence holding that a complete ban on abortion is unconstitutional.

The most troublesome aspect of *Roe* was not its provision of some protection for abortion but the specific system of protection it adopted. In the first trimester, the Court allowed very little regulation except to ensure that the abortion was performed properly. In the second trimester, the Court allowed more rigorous regulation to ensure the safety of abortions. The Court concluded that the state's interest became compelling in the third trimester "because the fetus then presumably has the capability of meaningful life outside the mother's womb." Thus, in the third trimester, abortions could be limited to those needed to protect the mother's life or health.

To some extent, any effort to accommodate conflicting interests will involve drawing somewhat arbitrary lines, as the Justices seem to have realized at the time.[4] But the trimester system seems more arbitrary than most, with only a single sentence in the opinion to justify it. By trying to lay down a comprehensive rule to govern all abortions in a single opinion, the Court was stretching its own capacity to foresee and intelligently analyze the various factual permutations that could arise in later cases. It was also asking later judges to follow its language with slavish precision, rather than leaving those judges any room to include their own thoughts in the development of abortion law. It is little wonder that this aspect of the decision was soon eroded[5] and ultimately rejected in *Casey*.[6]

Justice Potter Stewart privately faulted the Blackmun opinion for being "quite so inflexibly 'legislative'" in establishing the trimester system. A more flexible approach, such as the "undue burden" test later adopted in *Casey*, would have given the Court the opportunity to learn the facts it needed to reach a sound accommodation between women's rights and the countervailing state interest. A more flexible rule would also have allowed later judges to make their own contributions to abortion doctrine. But after interpreting old precedents as establishing broad principles, the Court seemed to want its new precedent to establish a rigid directive rather than a flexible principle.

INTERNATIONAL REFERENCE POINTS

In trying to assess the Court's work in this area, it is instructive to consider how the high courts of other countries have dealt with the abortion issue. The Canadian Supreme Court upheld the right to abortion in a 1988 case.[7] One of the judges observed that, at the most basic level, every pregnant woman is told by the anti-abortion law "that she cannot submit to a generally safe medical procedure that might offer clear benefit to her unless she meets criteria entirely unrelated to her own priorities and aspirations." The judge concluded that the anti-abortion law's procedural barriers "do not comport with the principles of fundamental justice."

Similarly, another Canadian judge stated that the "security of the person," which is protected by the Canadian Charter, "must include a right of access to medical treatment of a condition representing a danger to life or health without fear of criminal sanction." Although this judge conceded that protecting the fetus relates to concerns that are "pressing and substantial in a free and democratic society," that objective would not justify the severe breach of a woman's right to personal security. A third judge's opinion stressed that an "aspect of human dignity on which the Charter is founded is the right to make fundamental personal decisions without interference from the state." This judge emphasized that the decision whether to terminate a pregnancy "will have profound psychological, economic and social consequences for the pregnant woman" and that the decision "deeply reflects the way the woman thinks about herself and her relationship to others and to society as a whole."

The Canadian Supreme Court focused its analysis on the woman's rights. The German Constitutional Court's analysis provides a useful contrast, because it focuses on the fetus. A 1974 statute authorized abortion on demand in the first trimester of pregnancy. The Court found that this law violated the German constitution's imperative for the protection of human life. According to the Court, the woman's right to self-determination could not be the sole goal of the law. On the other hand, the government is not required to use the same methods to protect fetal life as other life. In particular, there were limits to how much the government can properly force a woman to sacrifice her own interests to protect the fetus. Hence, abortion remained permissible when the woman's life or health were seriously at risk or when the child would be deformed.

Notably, the German Court consciously decided not to follow the trend toward abortion liberalization elsewhere because of the special circumstances of German history. In light of the experience of the Nazi years, to which the German Constitution was a response, German law could not afford to take the risk of accepting any action that could appear to undervalue human life.

As a more recent opinion makes clear, the German government not only has a duty to protect fetal life, it also has a constitutional duty to minimize the extent to which pregnancy would place unreasonable demands on women. The government must ensure that women are able to afford to support their children and that women do not suffer from occupational or educational disadvantages because of childbearing. The government is also entitled to consider that counseling may actually be more effective than criminal sanctions, given the difficulty of criminal enforcement. Except where acceptable reasons for abortion exist, the government cannot routinely reimburse women for the cost of an abortion. However, it can still pay abortion costs for indigent women who cannot afford them, because otherwise those women might resort to cheaper illegal abortions, eliminating any chance that counseling would change their minds.

In some ways the German decisions are even more instructive than the Canadian one. In one direction, the German court has gone well beyond anything that conservative U.S. judges have advocated. Those American judges generally hold that the Constitution places no limits on state legislation regarding abortion. Hence, in their view, just as states have the right to ban all abortions, states can legalize abortion on demand if they want to; the German courts have forbidden the legalization of all abortions. Yet, in another sense, the German decision is much more sensitive to the rights of the pregnant woman than are American conservative jurists. The German Court has analyzed the issue as involving conflicting constitutional rights, holding the woman's right to be less dominant but still worthy of respect. Rather than being blithely willing to impose unwanted pregnancy on women, the German courts have sought to ensure that the burden is not excessive.

The system embraced by the German court may give higher weight to fetal rights than would be justifiable in our system. After all, the Germans were in part responding to the special demands of their own historical experience, one that is not shared by the United States. But what is most striking is that, even within the context of rulings that provide constitutional protection to the "right to life," the German courts have provided far more protection to women than the abortion restrictions advocated by American "right to life" advocates.

The abortion issue involves a difficult balance. All of the U.S. abortion rulings—including *Roe v. Wade* itself—have acknowledged that the state has a valid interest in protecting fetal life. Yet, as both the American decisions and those from Germany and Canada acknowledge, abortion restrictions can intrude heavy-handedly into women's lives by demanding that they accept extreme personal risks or extraordinary child-rearing burdens. Although it is difficult to be confident about where exactly the balance should be struck, what does seem obvious is that the government cannot simply ignore the woman's side of the equation. The U.S. courts have often been faced with abortion laws that give little or no weight to women's interests. They are harshly punitive, fail to make exceptions that most people would think were warranted, and unlike the German law, fail to provide economic and social support for women faced with the burdens of child rearing. Wherever the ideal balance may be, these laws not only fail to find it but give little evidence of trying.

On the whole, the U.S. Supreme Court seems to have struck a defensible balance in its decisions. Reproductive rights are clearly protected as human rights. In the United States, for example, few people would support either bans on contraceptives or laws that compelled abortions. Even in *Roe v. Wade*, the Supreme Court also recognized that there is a potentially strong countervailing govern-mental interest in preventing unnecessary abortions. Justice Kennedy and his two allies later established the "undue burden" test as a way of balancing these considerations. This test properly recog-nizes the existence of abortion rights but provides room for reason-able regulation.

Even if *Roe*'s recognition of a broad right to abortion was wrong, the Court was right in *Casey* when it refused to overrule *Roe*'s core holding that some right to an abortion exists. First, *Roe* does not sat-isfy the normal tests the Court uses to justify overruling. If it was wrong, it was not egregiously wrong. It had not been undermined by later decisions, and the Court had not found its test unworkable. And apart from direct reliance on the *Roe* opinion by doctors and by millions of women, it had also reshaped the political landscape in ways that would be difficult to undo. Thus, the normal standards for following precedent weighed against overruling *Roe*.

Despite all the attention that *Roe* has received from pro-life forces, it is not clear that overruling it would go very far to advance their goal of eliminating abortions. Even when abortions were illegal, the laws were virtually unenforceable; indeed, studies suggest that al-most as many illegal abortions occurred before *Roe* as legal abortions immediately after *Roe*. Some states would surely retain abortion rights under their own laws even if the Supreme Court stepped out of the picture. I doubt that we would emulate Ireland in bringing criminal prosecutions against women who try to leave the jurisdic-tion to get an abortion, and even Ireland has been brought up short by rulings that this policy violates the right to free travel. So most women—at least those who are not too young, poor, or disabled—would simply travel to the states where abortion is allowed.

Overruling *Roe* at this point would be more than a correction of an erroneous judicial opinion. It would be seen by the public as a major defeat for the Court as a guardian, even if sometimes an overzealous guardian, of individual rights. The Bork confirmation hearings made it clear how well accepted the concept of fundamental rights has become. Subsequent nominees have been careful not to take issue with *Griswold*. For the Court to abandon one of its most important decisions upholding individual rights, while under intense political fire and soon after major personnel changes, would be too much of an abdication of its independence and institutional role.

No doubt there is room for a fine-tuning of *Roe* and *Casey*. The precise balance cast by the Court is subject to reassessment based on further thought and new information. It would be a mistake, however, for the Court to repudiate the basic principle that women are entitled to *some* access to abortion. And any fine-tuning should be cautious, for even if the Court could have reasonably struck a different balance in its past decisions, respect for precedent places a considerable burden on those who seek to restrike the balance.

Of course, what I have written here is unlikely to end the debate over the constitutionality of abortion restrictions. Because of the weight of the opposing government interests, abortion cases are among the most difficult of fundamental rights cases. It is no wonder that they are also among the most controversial. Other cases are easier to decide under the approach I am advocating. Whether the subject is the right of terminal patients to refuse unwanted medical treatment or the right of a child to a basic education, the constitutional analysis turns out to be quite straightforward.

13

The End of Life

The Supreme Court has dealt gingerly with the topic of the right to die, and any recognition of this right must be tempered with an appreciation of the potential problems. The government clearly has the right to block decisions caused by mental illness, lack of information, or undue pressures. When the person is incapacitated, careful procedures are warranted to determine his or her true wishes. But at the end of the day, the Ninth Amendment does not allow the government to impose its own views on unwilling citizens.

These life-and-death issues are admittedly difficult. Consider the case of Kenneth Bergstedt.[1] He was a thirty-one-year-old with quadriplegia, who had become paralyzed at age ten as the result of a swimming accident. (A girl had jumped into the pool on top of him.) Faced with the impending death of his father, who had been his caretaker and constant companion, he no longer wanted to live. He petitioned the Washington State courts for an order allowing the removal of his respirator and administration of a sedative while he died.

Though the facts are not completely clear, before Bergstedt's case was decided by the Washington Supreme Court, his father apparently had decided not to wait for judicial approval before fulfilling his son's request. The father died a few days later. Nevertheless, the court decided the case in order to give future guidance.

The majority concluded that the request should have been granted as an exercise of a competent adult's fundamental right to refuse unwanted medical care. As the court explained, after his mother died, Bergstedt was entirely dependent on his father's help for all of his bodily functions, as well as for the limited sources of entertainment he could access. He feared that some accident might take place after his father's death, leaving him to suffocate agonizingly if his respirator failed. He was, in short, consumed by fear.

The majority thought this was an appropriate case to apply the principle that at some point "the present or prospective quality of life may be so dismal" that the right to reject life support prevails over the state's interest in protecting life. The court did not view this as a case of assisted suicide, but rather as the removal of the "artificial barriers standing between him" and death. For future cases, the court established an elaborate set of guidelines, including examination by two non-attending physicians to ensure that a patient's decision was knowing and voluntary.

A dissenting judge admitted that he had agonized over the case. "At one moment," he said, "I am haunted by the picture of a hopeless, wretched and tortured person who has no desire except to end his suffering by ending his life." He was concerned that Kenneth's death wish might have been prompted by an inadequate support system or by depression. But regardless of any factual dispute, he felt that the judicial branch was not the appropriate forum for considering these issues. In his view, "there was nothing natural about Mr. Bergstedt's death; he killed himself." Thus, he considered the case to be closer to assisted suicide than to the conventional right-to-die case where a person is in a coma or facing imminent death.

The U.S. Supreme Court has had a great deal of trouble with these issues about the end of life. Although the issues are very emotional and individual cases like Bergstedt's can be difficult to decide, it seems to me that there are two clear principles. The first is that competent adults have a fundamental right to refuse medical treatment and to control whether and when they receive treatment if they become incompetent. The second is that there is no fundamental right to assisted suicide.

THE RIGHT TO TERMINATE TREATMENT

The U.S. Supreme Court first encountered the issue of the right to die in *Cruzan*.[2] It seemed to be afraid to take a firmer position on the issue. Perhaps, if the Court had been able to rely on the stronger foundation of Ninth Amendment rights rather than the shaky basis of the Due Process Clause, it would have been willing to take a stronger stand.

A Missouri woman, Nancy Beth Cruzan, had been severely injured in a car crash and was in a persistent vegetative state. Having given up hope that she would ever regain consciousness, her parents sought a court order in state court to take her off life support. The trial judge had issued an order to remove her feeding tube, but the request was opposed by John Ashcroft, who was then the governor. The state supreme court reversed the trial court and announced that "clear and convincing evidence" of the patient's intention would be required. The case then went up to the U.S. Supreme Court.

The Court carefully reviewed a host of state cases, devoting pages of its opinion to reciting the facts and legal rulings of state supreme courts from Massachusetts, New York, New Jersey, and Illinois. The Court concluded that the "common-law doctrine of informed consent is viewed as generally encompassing the right of a competent individual to refuse medical treatment." Hence, the Court was willing to assume for purposes of the case that such a constitutional right did exist. As Chief Justice Rehnquist delicately put it, the "principle that a competent person has a constitutionally protected liberty interest in refusing unwanted medical treatment may be inferred from our prior decisions." Note the use of the passive voice here; he apparently was not quite willing to say that he himself would make this inference, just that someone else might do so.

However, even assuming the existence of a liberty interest, Rehnquist found no constitutional violation on the specific facts presented in this case. He upheld the Missouri court's ruling that required clear and convincing evidence of an incompetent patient's wish to withdraw life-sustaining treatment. Hence, in the absence of additional evidence, Cruzan would have to stay on life support.

Justice Scalia thought that Rehnquist had given too much credit to the right to die. "I would have preferred," he said, "that we announce, clearly and promptly, that the federal courts have no business in this field; that American law has always accorded the State the power to prevent, by force if necessary, suicide—including suicide by refusing to take appropriate measures necessary to preserve one's life." The Court's opinion on Cruzan's situation was, he added, worth no more than that of "nine people picked at random from the Kansas City telephone directory." His concluding sentence was that the Court had no authority to "inject itself into every field of human activity where irrationality and oppression may theoretically occur, and if it tries do so it will destroy itself."

Justice Brennan's dissent seemed to have the better of the argument. He was less coy than Rehnquist about the existence of a constitutionally protected right. Brennan had no hesitancy in stating that the right to be "free from medical attention without consent, to determine what shall be done with one's own body, *is* deeply rooted in this Nation's traditions." He faulted the state for putting a heavy burden on the parents to prove their daughter would not have wanted the life support to continue, rather than simply trying to make the most accurate determination possible of what she would have wanted. In effect, the state was presuming that most people would want to remain on life support forever while in an irreversible coma.

Another dissent, by Justice Stevens, is one of the few occasions that a Supreme Court Justice has quoted the Declaration of Independence in recent years. He said that the "Constitution is born of the proposition that all legitimate governments must secure the equal right of every person to 'Life, Liberty, and the pursuit of Happiness.'" He could see no reason to uphold the state's abstract interest in the preservation of biological life at the expense of what the trial court had found to be her own previous wishes. In his view, the state wished to require continued life support as a symbolic expression of its commitment to human life, a noble commitment but one it was not entitled to express by appropriating her life as a symbol.

As it turned out, the Supreme Court's opinion was not the final word on Cruzan's situation. Three close friends of Cruzan came forward with evidence that she would want the tube removed. The lower court then ruled this was clear and convincing evidence, and the decision was not appealed. Her feeding tube was removed six months after the Supreme Court's decision. Fifteen members of Operation Rescue appeared at the hospital to reinsert the feeding tube, but they were arrested. Cruzan died eleven days later.

ASSISTED SUICIDE

The Court has also addressed the more contentious issue of assisted suicide.[3] State laws have generally banned physicians from providing patients with prescription drugs to use to end their lives, even if the patients have no prospect of regaining any semblance of recovery. At the time, these bans were universal in the United States (though Oregon has more recently allowed assisted suicide under some circumstances). In the international context, Holland was the main exception. Chief Justice Rehnquist again wrote the majority opinion.

Citing the *Cruzan* opinion, he said that the Court had "assumed, and strongly suggested, that the Due Process Clause protects the traditional right to refuse unwanted lifesaving medical treatment." But Rehnquist also noted that the Court had been reluctant to expand the category of fundamental rights, for "guidelines for responsible decisionmaking in this uncharted area are scarce and open-ended." Although many constitutionally protected rights are connected with the idea of personal autonomy, he added, this "does not warrant the sweeping conclusion that any and all important, intimate, and personal decisions are so protected."

Rehnquist described a two-part analysis to determine the existence of a fundamental right: a "careful description" of the exact right involved, combined with an inquiry into whether the right is "deeply rooted in this Nation's history and tradition" and "implicit in the concept of ordered liberty." Rather than such a historical basis, Rehnquist found the opposite: the history of the legal responses to assisted suicide in this country has been one of almost complete rejection.

Chief Justice Rehnquist also pointed to empirical evidence about the Dutch practice that raised some question as to whether assisted suicide could be effectively limited to competent, terminally ill adults, or whether it might tend to expand in practice. A Dutch study had uncovered evidence that euthanasia had in fact not been limited to competent, terminally ill adults in severe pain, and that there may have been abuses in cases involving newborns with severe disabilities and elderly people with Alzheimer's disease. Given this uncertainty, there was much room for legitimate debate about the issue.

Rehnquist concluded by handing the issue back to the political process: "Throughout the Nation, Americans are engaged in an earnest and profound debate about the morality, legality, and practicality of physician-assisted suicide. Our holding permits this debate to continue, as it should in a democratic society."

The thrust of the ruling was somewhat blunted by Justice Sandra Day O'Connor's concurring opinion. As was often the case during her tenure on the Court, she was the swing voter. Four other members of the Court agreed with the result but thought the Court's opinion was too stringent. Justice O'Connor joined the majority opinion, but she emphasized that the distinction between assisted suicide and legitimate medical care was a thin one. In New York and Washington, the specific states involved in the case, a terminal patient who is in great pain can obtain necessary pain medication "even to the point of causing unconsciousness and hastening death." As long as the avowed purpose is pain prevention rather than suicide, the patient's death (desired as it may be) is a side effect rather than a goal.

So far, Oregon is the only state to provide for assisted suicide. The Oregon Death With Dignity Act allows any person with a terminal disease to make a written request to end his or her life "in a humane and dignified manner." The statute provides elaborate procedural safeguards. For example, it requires two witnesses to the written request (neither of whom can be a relative, stand to inherit, or be connected with the person's health care provider). There is also a waiting period before the request can be honored. In 2003, thirty-nine Oregonians took advantage of this provision, obtained prescriptions for lethal doses of medication, and died; another twenty-eight received the prescriptions but ultimately did not use them. The experience in Oregon suggests that the most likely patients to take lethal doses were those who were single, well-educated, and suffering from ALS, AIDS, or terminal cancer.

Attorney General Ashcroft, despite the Bush administration's avowed belief in states' rights, tried to stop Oregon by claiming that the use of prescription medications for this purpose violated federal law. His argument was ultimately rejected by the Supreme Court, which found that he lacked the authority to make this determination.

The Oregon approach may turn out to be the wave of the future. In the meantime, however, there seems to be clearly too little foundation for declaring any constitutional right to assisted suicide. On the other hand, there is clear support for a right to refuse unwanted medical treatment. Some philosophers regard this as an illusory distinction: dead is dead. But it seems to correspond to deeply felt and widely shared intuitions. Whatever the law *should* be, it seems clear that both in the U.S. and internationally, we are far from recognizing a right to assisted suicide. As Justice Holmes was wont to say, the life of the law is not logic but experience.

Oregon's efforts may help clear up some unanswered questions about assisted suicide: Will it encourage resort to this measure when psychiatric treatment or better pain management could alleviate the patient's problems? Will vulnerable populations like people of color and people with disabilities be disproportionately involved in the practice? To what extent will the availability of assisted suicide simply steer people who would have committed suicide anyway to a less painful method? How well-informed and truly voluntary will decisions for assisted suicide really be?

Thus, the Oregon experience promises to teach us a great deal about the potential benefits and abuses of assisted suicide. One of the boasts of our system of federalism is that it makes the states laboratories of experimentation with new approaches to social problems. It was wrong for Ashcroft to try to use the federal drug laws to halt the experiment. But allowing the experiment in a single, willing state is one thing; using the courts to foist it on the entire nation is another. Clearly, the time is not ripe to consider this a constitutional right, and perhaps it never will be.

This leaves two questions. One is line drawing. Recall the story of Kenneth Bergstedt, recounted at the beginning of this chapter. Was he simply seeking to reject medical treatment (a protected right under *Cruzan*), or was he seeking assisted suicide (not a protected right)? It seems to me that the majority in the Washington Supreme Court had the correct answer: it was a refusal of treatment case. Generally, a mentally competent, fully informed adult would have the right to reject in advance the use of a respirator. Having temporarily given permission, a person should be entitled to a change of heart. If agreeing to a respirator or other intrusive procedures was irrevocable, people might be reluctant to say yes in the first place for fear they were agreeing to a life sentence. More fundamentally, to say that people are obligated to tolerate the intrusion of breathing tubes and the mechanical performance of a critical life function solely to provide an example of how society values life would be to say in some sense that they do not possess their own bodies. The state may have no obligation to help someone die, but at least an individual should be able to insist on being left alone rather than being used as an exhibit to promote social values.

The second question is whether there should be some exceptions, so that under some more limited circumstances there *would* be a right to assisted suicide. For example, what about a person in permanent, agonizing pain? Perhaps Justice O'Connor is right that the constitutional issue here can be avoided by pretending that a dangerous dose of medication is simply designed to suppress pain for awhile. However, this seems an unsatisfying solution to the extent that it solves the problem only by ignoring reality. My own sympathies would be strongly in favor of assisted suicide under these circumstances. It remains unclear, however, whether there is enough legal or social consensus even under these special circumstances to make this a constitutional right.

14

Gay Rights

Gay people were a reviled minority for much of the twentieth century. Toward the turn of the century, courts began to recognize their constitutional rights. This is an important vindication of the notion of fundamental rights that underlies the Ninth Amendment. Today, the battlefield has shifted to same-sex marriage. Although the two legal areas are superficially similar, I believe that from a constitutional viewpoint they are quite different.

HOMOSEXUAL ACTS

The initial issue that the Supreme Court had to decide was whether homosexual sex could be outlawed. It first encountered this issue twenty years ago, with results that were proved unsatisfactory.

Bowers v. Hardwick[1] involved the prosecution of a Georgia man who was discovered having oral sex with another man when the police broke into the bedroom of his house to execute a search warrant. The Court conceded that the "cases are legion" in which the Due Process Clause had been interpreted to protect substantive rights, including some that had "little or no textual support in the constitutional language." But the Court said only rights "deeply rooted in this Nation's history and tradition" could qualify for such protection. It assured itself that what it called "homosexual sodomy" did not have the blessing of such a tradition. The majority ruled against the defendant.

In dissent, Justice Blackmun argued that "individuals define themselves in a significant way through their intimate sexual relationships with others." He believed that in a country as diverse as America, there "may be many 'right' ways of conducting the relationships," so that "much of the richness of a relationship will come from the freedom an individual has to *choose* the form and nature of these intensely personal bonds." In Justice Blackmun's view, "only the most willful obstinacy" could obscure the fact that sexuality is a key human activity, central to family life, community welfare, and the development of human personality.

In a separate dissenting opinion, Justice Stevens observed that sexual activities of married couples were clearly constitutionally protected and that existing precedent showed that similar protection extended to unmarried opposite-sex couples. The Georgia statute was thus too broad. There was no evidence that the Georgia legislature meant to single out a subcategory of acts by same-sex couples, and no reason except possible animus against gays to think that they would want to do so. Hence, Stevens said, the whole statute should be regarded as unenforceable.

The *Bowers* majority may have been a little overconfident in its assessment of American legal traditions. At least until the twentieth century, laws banning "crimes against nature" were not specifically targeted at male homosexuals, and the laws probably did not cover lesbians at all. The common law did not regard oral sex as a crime against nature. According to a careful historical study, "as late as 1879, there was no authoritative American statute or judicial decision disagreeing with the common law rule that oral sex was not a crime against nature."[2] When the law shifted on that issue in the late nineteenth century, only a few states did so by judicial interpretation of their existing laws; most passed specific new laws. The cases from Georgia reflect how unsettled the law was: first the Georgia Supreme Court found oral sex to be a crime against nature in 1904; then it specifically ruled on fellatio but waffled on cunnilingus, first holding it to be a crime, then not a crime if between two women, and then finally not a crime for heterosexuals either. (There is a story, perhaps apocryphal, that nineteenth-century English sodomy laws did not cover lesbians because none of the Crown's ministers wished to undertake the task of explaining the issue to Queen Victoria.) None of this shows, of course, that there was a tradition viewing any of these sexual acts as constitutionally protected, but the history does show that legal condemnation of these acts was not deeply embedded.

The *Bowers* decision was not well received by constitutional scholars or by much of the legal community. For example, only a few years later, the Kentucky Supreme Court interpreted its state constitution to require a contrary result.[3] The Kentucky court called *Bowers* misdirected in its application of originalism and factually ignorant (in part because of the U.S. Supreme Court's lack of awareness of the history discussed above). The Kentucky court concluded: "'Equal Justice Under Law' inscribed above the entrance to the United States Supreme Court, expresses the unique goal to which all humanity aspires. In Kentucky it is more than a mere aspiration."

The U.S. Supreme Court's next encounter with gay rights was in a Colorado case, *Romer v. Evans*.[4] In 1992, Colorado voters ratified an amendment to the state constitution that effectively prohibited the state or any of its subdivisions from enacting laws that protect gay people from discrimination.

At first blush, there seemed to be three plausible arguments for invalidating the Colorado measure. First, it might deprive gays of a fundamental right, thus triggering (and failing) strict scrutiny under the Equal Protection Clause. This, in fact, was the basis for the Colorado court's decision. Second, it might be directed at a discrete and insular minority, again triggering some form of heightened scrutiny under the Equal Protection Clause. Although plaintiffs made this argument, and many commentators support it, none of the various courts in the litigation accepted it. Finally, the Supreme Court might have relied on cases that apply a somewhat stricter form of minimal scrutiny, sometimes called "rational basis with teeth." (For example, it used this approach to strike down a zoning ordinance that excluded group homes for people with mental retardation.) In fact, the Supreme Court did none of these things. Instead, the Court announced that the Colorado measure failed to satisfy even the most minimal scrutiny, which involves the barest requirement of a passable but not necessarily plausible justification for a law. Nevertheless, the Court seemed to be applying a more stringent test without saying so.

The Court's puzzling analysis left it vulnerable to a blistering dissent by Justice Scalia. Justice Scalia argued that the rational basis test was easily met. If a state can make homosexual conduct a crime, "surely it is constitutionally permissible for a State to enact other laws merely disfavoring homosexual conduct." Furthermore, if it is rational to criminalize the conduct, surely it is rational to deny special favor and protection to those with a self-avowed tendency or desire to engage in the conduct. Indeed, according to Justice Scalia, where criminal sanctions are not involved, homosexual "orientation" is an acceptable stand-in for homosexual conduct. Thus, Justice Scalia concluded, "no principle set forth in the Constitution, nor even any imagined by this Court in the past 200 years, prohibits what Colorado has done here." Accusing the majority of relying on its own sense of righteousness rather than precedent, Justice Scalia characterized the decision as an imposition of elite cultural values on the populace. The majority, he said, had confused a culture war with a Kulturkampf.

If, as Justice Scalia so forcibly argued, the *Romer* opinion is inde-fensible on its own terms, is there any explanation for the opinion other than sheer lawlessness? One possible argument is that the Court correctly concluded that no group—whether gays, smokers, left-handers, or the overweight—can be labeled by the government as pariahs. Even when the government has the power to criminalize certain conduct, it still does not have unlimited authority to pro-mote private discrimination against any group with a propensity to engage in that conduct. By creating a constitutional right to discrim-inate against one—and only one—group in society, Colorado had branded gays as a pariah group.

In retrospect, the Colorado decision can be seen as a stepping-stone toward overruling *Bowers*. The premise of Justice Scalia's dis-sent was that the state was entitled to outlaw homosexual conduct, an assumption that was sustained by the *Bowers* ruling. Perhaps Jus-tice Kennedy, the author of the Colorado decision, already had doubts on this score, but was not yet willing to take the drastic step of overruling such a recent decision as *Bowers*.

If so, he did not have to wait long for another opportunity. The new case came from Texas. After a reported weapons disturbance, Texas police entered the apartment of a man named John Lawrence and discovered him having sex with another man. Lawrence was ar-rested for violating a Texas law banning "deviate [*sic*] sexual inter-course with another individual of the same sex." Texas defines deviate sexual intercourse to include oral and anal sex. Lawrence was convicted and fined $200 plus court costs. He appealed through the Texas courts, which affirmed the conviction on the basis of *Bow-ers*. Then he took his case to the U.S. Supreme Court.

Justice Kennedy wrote the majority opinion to overrule *Bowers*.[5] He characterized the state law as "touching upon the most private human conduct, sexual behavior, and in the most private of places, the home." He cautioned against the government setting bound-aries on sexual conduct "absent injury to a person or abuse of an institution the law protects." Kennedy also observed that the *Bowers* Court had gotten its history wrong. Traditional "crimes against nature" included opposite-sex as well as same-sex conduct. It was only in the 1970s that some states began to single out same-sex relations for criminal punishment, and only nine states had done so. Other states had moved to repeal or invalidate their bans on anal and oral sex. Five states had declined to follow *Bowers* in interpreting their own state constitutions.

Justice Kennedy emphasized that five years before *Bowers*, the European Court of Human Rights considered the case of a gay man in Northern Ireland, which prohibited same-sex relations. The court held that the laws against this conduct violated the European Convention on Human Rights. The ECHR has authority within what are now the forty-five members of the Council of Europe. In its initial encounter with the issues, several years before *Bowers*, the ECHR characterized Irish anti-sodomy legislation as a continuing interference with an individual's right to respect for his private life.[6] The court could find no pressing social need for such an intrusion on "an essentially private manifestation of the human personality."

Later European decisions are also instructive. The European court reaffirmed its ruling against Ireland in 1988. In 1986, the European Commission had also determined that setting the age of consent for homosexual activities higher than that for heterosexual activities violated the Convention. However, the right to private sexual behavior, even between consenting adults, is not absolute: a 1997 case held that the state could restrict sadomasochistic practices that caused significant injuries.

Justice Kennedy also pointed out that *Bowers* had been undermined by later decisions. One of those decisions was the Colorado case, which we have just discussed. The other was *Casey*, which reaffirmed *Roe. v. Wade*, thereby reinforcing that matters involving the "most intimate and personal choices a person may make in a lifetime, choices central to personal dignity and autonomy, are central" to the Fourteenth Amendment's protection of liberty. It might have been truer to history if the Court had spoken instead of that amendment's P or I Clause, and doing so might have provided better ammunition against critics of the decision.

Justice Scalia dissented. He accused the majority of invalidating, by implication, states' laws against bigamy, same-sex marriage, adult incest, prostitution, masturbation (yes, he really said that), adultery, fornication, bestiality, and obscenity. After all, these were all "morals" laws just like bans on homosexuality. He said it was clear that the Court had taken sides in the culture wars by dismissing the views of Americans who did not want gays as business partners, scoutmasters, schoolteachers, or tenants. "So imbued is the Court with the law profession's anti-anti-homosexual culture, that it is seemingly unaware that the attitudes of that culture are not obviously 'mainstream.'" He also criticized the Court for citing foreign legal authorities, which he called irrelevant to our own national history and traditions.

In short, according to Scalia, the majority's opinion was "the product of a Court, which is the product of a law-profession culture that has largely signed on to the so-called homosexual agenda." Justice Scalia ended by warning that gay marriage was a necessary byproduct of the majority's decision. That conclusion could be avoided only "if one entertains the belief that principle and logic have nothing to do with the decisions of this Court."

Justice Scalia's views notwithstanding, reason was on the side of Justice Kennedy. Kennedy was clearly right that homosexual sodomy laws violate the modern understanding of human rights. Such laws have been largely repudiated within the United States, by legislatures elsewhere, and by courts in countries such as South Africa. In addition, respected international bodies have found that homosexual relations are protected from government interference.

Aside from the ECHR decision discussed earlier, for example, the Human Rights Committee has found that anti-sodomy laws violated the International Covenant on Civil and Political Rights (which the United States has ratified). In arguing otherwise, Justice Scalia and his supporters are simply ignoring a conclusion that the rest of civilization has long since accepted.

SAME-SEX MARRIAGE

As Justice Scalia pointed out, the Court in the Texas *Lawrence* case had carefully withheld judgment about same-sex marriage. The Court said that the case before it "does not involve whether the government must give formal recognition to any relationship that homosexual persons seek to enter." But same-sex marriage is an issue that sooner or later is likely to require guidance from the Court.

Up until now, most of the action has been in the state courts, applying state rather than federal constitutions. A state can establish broader rights under its own constitution than the Supreme Court reads into the federal Constitution, so these state decisions are not subject to review by the Court.

The issue of gay marriage received serious judicial sanction for the first time in a 1993 decision by the Hawaii Supreme Court, which applied the state constitution to the issue.[7] The court considered restrictions on same-sex marriage to be a kind of gender discrimination. Obviously, under conventional laws, who you can marry depends on the gender of the person involved (as well as your own). The court sent the case back to the trial level for a determination of whether the state could present a sufficient justification for this sex discrimination. The lower court judge found no such justification. The Hawaii Supreme Court had relied only on the state constitution, but while the case was on appeal, the voters overwhelmingly approved a state constitutional amendment. The state amendment authorized the legislature to define marriage to include only opposite-sex couples. That was the end of the Hawaii case, but not of the issue of same-sex marriage.

Yes, there *is* a right to marry. The ability to decide who to marry or who not to marry is a key part of "owning your own life." Indeed, the only adults in American history who have been completely denied this right were those who were literally owned by others—African American slaves.

The right to marry achieved constitutional recognition in the 1967 case of *Loving v. Virginia*.[8] A Virginia statute prohibited interracial marriage. Besides finding the statute unconstitutional because it discriminated on the basis of race, the Court also held that it was an unconstitutional violation of liberty. As the Court said, the "freedom to marry has long been recognized as one of the vital personal rights essential to the orderly pursuit of happiness by free men"—"one of the 'basic civil rights of man,' fundamental to our very existence and survival."

Freedom to marry was no invention of the Warren Court. Even in the Middle Ages, the *ius communus* (equivalent to the later "law of nations") recognized the right to be free from forced marriage. At the time, the issue was not coercion by the government but coercion by families through arranged marriage. Marriages entered into under coercion could be dissolved.[9]

The constitutional status of marriage was confirmed in two important later decisions. A 1978 ruling overturned a Wisconsin law that prohibited remarriage by anyone with overdue support obligations from a past marriage.[10] Justice Thurgood Marshall remarked that it is "not surprising that the decision to marry has been placed on the same level of importance as decisions relating to procreation, childbirth, child rearing, and familial relationships." He added that it "would make little sense to recognize a right to privacy with respect to other matters of family life and not with respect to the decision to enter into a relationship that is the foundation of the family in our society." The Wisconsin law infringed on this right unnecessarily, since Wisconsin could use other methods to ensure that child support was paid.

Nine years later, the Court reaffirmed the right to marriage in a unanimous decision written by Justice O'Connor. A state regulation prohibited prison inmates to marry. The Court held that the right to marry was valid even in prison settings, where sex with outsiders is normally prohibited. According to Justice O'Connor, "inmate marriages, like others, are expressions of emotional support and public commitment." Also, because many religions view marriage as having spiritual significance, the commitment of marriage may be "an exercise of religious faith as well as an expression of personal dedication." And most inmates will eventually be released, so couples can reasonably expect that the marriages will someday be consummated. And finally, marital status is keyed to many government benefits, which remain relevant even to prisoners. Thus, excluding prisoners from the right to marry was unacceptable unless it was reasonably related to legitimate penological objectives. Justice O'-Connor could find no such reasonable relationship.

The right to marry seems firmly established, although its foundations in the Constitution are disputed. For those leery of reading substance into the Due Process Clause, the Ninth Amendment (and its cousin, the P or I Clause) provides a more satisfactory foundation for this right. The Ninth comes in handy here—for example, easily invalidating laws against interracial marriage.

The big issue today, obviously, is gay marriage. From one perspective, current law clearly restricts the freedom to choose a marriage partner; it has to be someone of the opposite sex. From another perspective, a marriage partner by definition has to be someone of the opposite sex; otherwise it is not really a marriage.

What the Ninth Amendment can contribute to this debate is not a clear-cut answer, but rather directions about where to look for an answer. To determine whether the right to choose a marital partner extends past gender lines, we need to take into account the views of state and federal legislators, state courts, and international authorities.

At present, the idea of same-sex marriage as a fundamental right does not seem to be taking hold. Compare the situation with *Lawrence*, the Texas sodomy case. In terms of gay marriage, unlike sodomy laws, legislation against the practice cannot be considered superannuated, a minority view among states, or subject to a trend toward repeal. Nearly all the state courts to hear such cases have rejected gay marriage claims. Congress has passed legislation authorizing states to ignore same-sex marriages entered into in other states, in a statute tellingly entitled the "Defense of Marriage Act."

There is also sparse international legislation supporting a fundamental right to same-sex marriage and no rulings by human rights tribunals. The European Human Rights Convention protects the "right to marry and to found a family," but only for heterosexual couples. Indeed, the ECHR has held that even after surgery, transsexuals are not entitled to marry members of their former gender. Lower courts in Canada have held that same-sex couples must be allowed to marry, but they seem to have based their rulings primarily on the Canadian Charter's broad prohibition of discriminatory laws, not on a fundamental rights analysis. The issue did not reach the Canadian Supreme Court because the government chose not to appeal. In short, in terms of the existence of some kind of consensus, even an emerging consensus, gay marriage is far different from the sodomy issue.

What is perhaps the most striking evidence is that even the three state courts that to date have supported gay marriage (or civil union) have not found it to be a fundamental right. In the Hawaii case discussed earlier, the state court expressly rejected that argument. Its analysis was based solely on the alleged presence of gender discrimination (because the right to marry depends on the sex of the partner).

In 1999, when the Vermont Supreme Court held that same-sex couples are entitled to all of the legal benefits of marital status (but not necessarily the name), it also avoided relying on a fundamental rights argument, instead applying a lesser level of review.[11] The court also explicitly rejected the Hawaii court's sex discrimination claim. The Vermont court accepted the validity of the state's purported goals, such as promoting commitment between married couples to promote security for children. But the Court held that excluding same-sex couples from marriage had no reasonable relationship to that goal. Expressing some concern about the potentially destabilizing effect of its ruling, the Court allowed the existing statutory scheme to stay in effect a reasonable amount of time to allow the legislature to enact new laws on the subject. Notably, the court nowhere said that the state's law violated the fundamental right to marry.

Even more recently, in 2003, the highest court of Massachusetts went beyond the Vermont ruling, mandating not only recognition of civil unions but same-sex marriage.[12] Again, however, the fundamental rights argument was not the basis for decision. Instead, the court held that preclusion of same-sex marriage does not satisfy the "rational basis test." That test is the lowest level of constitutional scrutiny, applying to all government regulations whether they regulate intimate personal matters or the pricing of grain options.[13]

In a ruling only a few weeks ago as I write, New York's highest court rejected the Massachusetts view. According to the New York court, the legislature could rationally conclude that instability causes more serious problems in heterosexual unions, where children are most likely. This could be true either because same-sex relationships are less likely to lead to children, or that only the most stable same-sex relationships are likely to lead to children, so they do not need social reinforcement. Thus the legislature could conclude that the extra stability of legal marriage was most needed for heterosexual couples.

What all of this adds up to is that there is a plausible argument for defining marriage in terms of heterosexual couples that has nothing to do with bias against gays. This is not to say that the argument for same-sex marriage is lacking in moral appeal. Justice Scalia was wrong in thinking that the *Lawrence* decision inevitably meant legalization of gay marriage. But he was right that some of the moral underpinning of *Lawrence*, in terms of respect for intimate personal relations, may also speak to same-sex marriage. Criminalizing a relationship is much harsher, however, than refusing to give that relationship official recognition. As the dissent in the Massachusetts case pointed out, "the law always lags behind the most advanced thinking in every area," and judges must wait for "some common ground, some consensus." We may be heading toward an eventual consensus, but at this point, it would be hard to find firm grounding for a fundamental rights analysis of same-sex marriage.

Recall that not even the courts accepting arguments for same-sex marriage have been willing to explicitly include it within the existing constitutional right to marry. That answer may not stand for all eternity—and for what it is worth, I suspect that it will not. Social change in this area has been vigorous. As non-gay people come to know committed same-sex couples, they are unlikely to oppose formalizing such commitments. That may well be the direction of social policy. But courts should think twice before plunging so far ahead of current social thought.

15

Education

Education is necessary for an individual to participate fully in any modern society, politically as well as economically. The Supreme Court has acknowledged this fact but has not been willing to find education to be a fundamental right. With all due respect, the Court is simply wrong on this one.

RULINGS ON EDUCATION BY U.S. COURTS

In the 1973 *Rodriguez* ruling,[1] the Supreme Court rejected a challenge to the grossly unequal treatment of children in the Texas school system. For every $600 spent in the richest districts, less than $250 in state funds were spent in the poorest. Too bad, said the Supreme Court. The Court implied that, at most, there *might* be a fundamental right to the "minimal basic skills necessary for the rights of speech and of full participation in the political process." But Texas had managed to meet this very minimal standard, and the state did at least steer clear of "an absolute denial of educational opportunities to any of its children."

In his dissenting opinion, Justice Thurgood Marshall protested against the "majority's labored efforts to demonstrate that fundamental interests . . . encompass only established rights which we are somehow bound to recognize from the text of the Constitution it-self." As its text and history demonstrate, the Ninth Amendment, of course, rejects the idea that only the enumerated rights are pro-tected. As Marshall pointed out, the right to education is closely re-lated to the ability to exercise First Amendment rights; however, he protested in vain.

Thus, any recognized federal constitutional right to an education was deemed at most extremely narrow. About a decade later, a bare majority of the Court did strike down another Texas law, which de-nied schooling to children who had entered the country illegally with their parents.[2] The opinion, written by Justice Brennan, uses some broad language. For example, Justice Brennan said that educa-tion is not merely another government benefit like other forms of social welfare legislation because of "the importance of education in maintaining our basic institutions, and the lasting impact of its deprivation on the life of the child." Nevertheless, he reconfirmed that education is not a fundamental right. The unconstitutional fea-ture of the statute was its combination of two features: the com-plete deprivation of education and targeting a class of children who were not at fault and whose parents were politically powerless ille-gal aliens. Justices who had joined the earlier decision wrote concur-ring opinions to say that this law was different because it was an absolute denial of education to a defined group and threatened the creation of a permanent underclass.

At the state level, the constitutional picture is much different. Every state constitution contains a requirement for public educa-tion. Many state courts have interpreted either this clause or more general provisions of their own constitutions to provide far greater protection to education. Texas itself embraced a broad right of edu-cational equality in a 1989 opinion of the state supreme court. The resulting educational reforms in Texas during the governorship of George W. Bush helped inspire the No Child Left Behind Act. By giving Bush a track record on education issues, the Texas court's decision may also have helped boost his 2000 presidential campaign.

A considerable number of state courts have issued decisions similar to the Texas ruling, beginning with the California Supreme Court in 1976. For example, the Vermont Supreme Court ruled that the existing system of education "has fallen short of providing every school-age child in Vermont an equal educational opportunity."[3] The Vermont court also commented that the "distribution of a resource as precious as educational opportunity may not have as its determining force the mere fortuity of a child's residence. It requires no particular constitutional expertise to recognize the capriciousness of such a system."

In 1989, the Kentucky Supreme Court issued a particularly influential ruling.[4] The court found the entire state system of education unconstitutional and ordered the state to undertake a complete overhaul. The opinion stressed the weakness of the Kentucky education system compared with neighboring states. The court set out guidelines for determining whether the educational system was adequate, including giving students sufficient communication skills, enough knowledge of societal issues to make informed choices, and the basis for choosing an occupation. Courts in New Hampshire, Alabama, and Massachusetts followed Kentucky's lead.

In response to the court's decision, the state enacted the Kentucky Education Reform Act, which moved Kentucky from the lowest rank of states in school spending up to the middle. The reforms resulted in a 25 percent spending increase in the poorest districts. It also created an assessment system, state curricular standards, and incentives for school performance.

An interesting contrast is provided by North Carolina, where the court has placed less emphasis on equalizing funding. The North Carolina Supreme Court has refused to hold that equality of financing between districts is required.[5] But its foundational opinion on the subject did not leave the field of education entirely to the discretion of the state legislature. There would be a case for judicial intervention, the court said, if the plaintiffs could provide clear evidence that some children were denied a "sound basic education." Under those circumstances, unless the government could show a compelling enough reason to deny the right—which seems almost impossible—the court would have to require "relief as needed to correct the wrong while minimizing the encroachment upon the other branches of government."

In fact, in a more recent opinion, the North Carolina court did find that the state school system flunked this test.[6] The finding of inadequacy was based on standardized test scores, dropout rates, lack of college preparation, and complaints from employers of the poor academic qualification of high school graduates. The state supreme court ordered the legislature to reconsider the amount of financial and other resources earmarked for disadvantaged schools.

The states are not in complete accord, but many leading courts have joined this movement toward recognizing the right to education. In 2002 alone, the highest courts of Tennessee, Arkansas, and New York affirmed this view. The Arkansas court emphasized the "dire need for changing the school funding system forthwith to bring it into constitutional compliance." The New York court demanded that the state provide a sound basic education, meaning the basic skills necessary to "function productively as civic participants capable of voting and sitting on a jury."

LESSONS FROM HISTORY AND FROM ABROAD

Historical research by my colleague Goodwin Liu shows that there is an especially strong basis for including education within the Fourteenth Amendment as an attribute of citizenship.[7] From 1866 to 1870, the Freedmen's Bureau (which was primarily formed to help freed slaves) spent over two-thirds of its funds on education, augmented by support from local governments and private donors. The year after the passage of the Fourteenth Amendment, Congress created a federal education department. Supporters argued that "every child of this land is, by natural right, entitled to an education." At the very least, they said, every child should receive enough of an education to perform the duties of citizenship. When proclaiming the ratification of the Fifteenth Amendment giving blacks the right to vote, President Ulysses Grant emphasized that "a republican form of government could not endure without intelligence and education generally diffused among the people."

In 1870, an effort was made to establish a national school system for states that did not have their own school systems. Those districts were primarily in the South, where public education had lagged. What is surprising is not that the bill failed but that it was proposed and seriously considered at all. The argument for passage was that education was necessary for citizenship and that the federal government had the inherent power to make sure this prerequisite was achieved. As the sponsor said, among the fundamental rights of a citizen, "by logical necessity, included the right to receive a full, free, ample education from the Government, in the administration of which it is his right and his duty to take an intelligent part."

Although this bill never went to a vote, a related piece of legislation would have applied the proceeds of public land sales to supporting public education. This bill passed the House and was enthusiastically endorsed by President Grant. However, it failed in the Senate because Senator Morrill wanted the money to go to land grant colleges rather than primary and secondary schools. (Having spent much of my career at two of those land grant colleges, the University of Minnesota and the University of Illinois, I feel a certain sympathy with Morrill's position.) Even though the proposed public school legislation never passed, it shows that the members of the

House, only six years after the passage of the Fourteenth Amendment, thought that education was a basic right of citizenship.

Although the Senate did not pass that bill, it repeatedly passed legislation in the 1880s on the subject of education. To receive federal funding, states would be required to provide a system of free public education to all children "without distinction of race or color." The debates on this proposal take up hundreds of pages in the *Congressional Record*. The committee report on the bill said that the federal government had the duty to educate the people of the United States for the duties of citizenship. Or, as one supporter said, if Congress has the right to protect voters from harassment in the use of the ballot (which the Supreme Court had upheld), "it must have the power to aid in preparing him for its intelligent use." In other words, without an education a voter "cannot be a citizen, at least not a useful citizen." This line of argument was made by others, and as Liu points out, there were few objections. Indeed, the bill passed the Senate by margins of up to two to one. Unfortunately, the House leadership kept it bottled up in committee even though it had wide support among the members.

In short, as Liu says, "leading proponents of federal aid understood the measures as an exercise of Congress's power and duty to enforce and give substance to the guarantee of American citizenship." This does not prove that Congress had a clearly formulated understanding about the relationship of citizenship and education when it enacted the Fourteenth Amendment. What it does prove is that finding education to be a fundamental right is entirely consistent with the thinking of the time.

It is also supported by the language of the Supreme Court's most important opinion of the twentieth century, *Brown v. Board of Education*.[8] *Brown* struck down school segregation in the South. On the way to that conclusion, Chief Justice Warren's opinion for a unanimous bench made some telling observations about the role of education, stressing the "importance of education to our democratic society." Warren added that education is "required in the performance of our most basic public responsibilities, even service in the armed forces," as well as being "the very foundation of good citizenship." Thus, he concluded, such "an opportunity, where the state has undertaken to provide it, is a right which must be made available to all on equal terms." It is a pity that the Court did not give more credence to this viewpoint twenty years later, when it rejected the fundamental right to an education in *Rodriguez*.

The fundamental right to education also has strong international support. Article 26 of the Universal Declaration of Human Rights provides that everyone has the right to an education, which should be "directed to the full development of the human personality and to the strengthening of respect for human rights and fundamental freedoms." Similarly, in Article 13, the International Covenant on Economic, Social, and Cultural Rights recognizes "the right of everyone to an education" sufficient to enable them to "participate effectively in a free society." The Covenant calls, where possible, for free education from grade school through college. Similarly, the South African constitution guarantees everyone the right to a basic education.

The European Convention on Human Rights also provides that no one may be denied the right to education. The European Court of Human Rights has interpreted this to restrict limitations on access to schooling. For example, in a bilingual country, where practical the government must make education in both languages available, since the right to an education would otherwise be meaningless to speakers of a minority tongue.[9]

As Cass Sunstein points out, most Americans probably accept the idea of education and similar basic rights. But people are skeptical that courts can enforce such rights, since they lack the power to manage or finance education.[10] And of course, there are real limits to how much courts can do to improve educational systems; they certainly cannot run them effectively. Yet many state courts have been undeterred and have fostered genuine improvements in their states' educational systems. For example, one study shows that litigation reduced spending inequalities between districts by one-fifth to one-third. Wealthy districts did not have to lower their spending; instead, poor districts raised their spending by about 10 percent. Overall educational spending in the state increased as a result of increased tax revenues.[11]

Courts and legislatures have also become increasingly more sophisticated in their remedies. Efforts to equalize expenditures per students in every district meet fierce political resistance and press to the very limits, if not beyond, of what courts can hope to achieve. But courts have shown greater flexibility. For example, in 1995, the Texas Supreme Court accepted state legislation that shifted school district boundaries in order to equalize the average value of assessed property and created a system for educational quality assessment. But the court was untroubled that some differences between districts would remain. The point, the court said, was to ensure an adequate educational opportunity, not to level all districts down to the lowest level.[12]

Where the state courts are already actively pursuing educational equality, there may be little reason for federal court intervention. This is not, however, true in every state. Moreover, understanding education as a fundamental right would also empower Congress, using its power to enforce the Fourteenth Amendment, to legislate more vigorously in this area. In addition, the Supreme Court's ruling in favor of the children of illegal immigrants may well be put to the test by state legislatures in the near future, given growing anti-immigration sentiment. A fundamental right to education would put an end to doubts about the unconstitutionality of such measures.

Recognizing a fundamental right to education could also have significance under the Ninth Amendment. Congress does have sole responsibility for schooling in some areas, such as the District of Columbia, and it is not clear that a minimum adequate education is being offered. Moreover, Congress may be tempted to reduce educational opportunities for the children of illegal immigrants. Unlike the states, Congress is not subject to any anti-discrimination rule against disfavoring aliens. However, it should still be possible for those aliens to claim the benefit of the Ninth Amendment's protection of a fundamental right to education.

At the end of the day, the point is simply that education is an indispensable part of a free society. The Supreme Court ought to recognize that fact. After all, everyone else does.

16

The Right to Government Protection

As early as Sir William Blackstone in the eighteenth century, personal security was recognized as a fundamental right. Blackstone defined this right as consisting of "a person's legal and uninterrupted enjoyment of his life, his limbs, his body, his health, and his reputation." Magna Charta's distant descendant, the Universal Declaration of Human Rights, says that everyone has the right to "security of person." The U.S. Supreme Court apparently does not agree.

The Supreme Court made its position clear in the tragic case of a young boy named Joshua DeShaney.[1] Joshua's story is worth telling in some detail. His father had been given custody of Joshua when his parents divorced. When Joshua was three years old, his father's second wife complained to the police that he had been beating Joshua. The Department of Social Services interviewed the father but dropped the investigation when he denied the allegations. A year later, Joshua was admitted to a local hospital with bruises and cuts. The doctor on duty suspected child abuse and reported the incident. The county then convened a child protection team, which decided that there was not enough evidence to keep him in government custody. The father entered into a voluntary agreement to receive counseling. The counseling apparently did not work, if it actually happened at all. A month later, ER workers called child protection again to report that he once more had suspicious injuries.

Over the next six months, Joshua's caseworker made visits to the house, during which she saw injuries on his head. She put a note in the file about her suspicions that Joshua was being abused, but she didn't do anything about it. Yet again, child protection was called by the ER for new injuries, which the ER workers attributed to child abuse. Child protection officers did nothing. The next two times a caseworker visited the house, she was told Joshua was too "ill" to see her. Neighbors reported to the police that they had seen or heard Joshua being abused by his father. There was still no action.

A few months later, Joshua's father beat him into a coma. Surgery showed that he had had a number of hemorrhages caused by a long series of head injuries. Joshua was expected to spend the rest of his life in an institution for people with profound mental retardation. The social worker had done nothing to intervene. Not that she was surprised, however. She said, "I just knew the phone would ring some day and Joshua would be dead."

Chief Justice Rehnquist, writing for the Court, explained that it was perfectly constitutional for the county to abandon Joshua to his father's violence. The Fourteenth Amendment, he said, confers "no affirmative right to governmental aid, even where such aid may be necessary to secure life, liberty, or property interests of which the government itself may not deprive the individual." Hence, "a State's failure to protect an individual against private violence simply does not constitute a violation of the Due Process Clause." Only when the state has actually taken a person into custody does it have a duty to protect that person from violence.

Too bad for Joshua: "While the State may have been aware of the dangers that Joshua faced in the free world, it played no part in their creation, nor did it do anything to render him any more vulnerable to them." In a nutshell, "the State had no constitutional duty to protect Joshua." If only Joshua had been a murderer serving a life sentence, he would have been entitled to protection as a person in state custody. As a mere innocent child, he had no such right.

Justice William Brennan, joined by Justice Thurgood Marshall, dissented. They argued that the state had intruded deeply enough in Joshua's life to make his situation analogous to government custody in terms of the government's responsibilities. In a brief, passionate dissent, Justice Harry Blackmun decried the boy's fate: "Poor Joshua! Victim of repeated attacks by an irresponsible, bullying, cowardly, and intemperate father" and then abandoned to his fate by state officials.

Despite the Court's brusque response to Joshua's situation, the right to government protection has a solid historical pedigree. In 1608, Sir Edward Coke spoke of a mutual bond between sovereign and subject. Within this bond, the subject owed allegiance, and the sovereign owed a duty to protect his subjects. Locke would explain in the following century that one of the main purposes of the social compact is to provide each individual with protection from injury and violence. Blackstone, too, said that "protection and subjection are reciprocal." As the 1780 Massachusetts constitution put it, each member of society has the right to its protection in his or her life, liberty, and property. Of course, not everyone had the right to protection: slaves were largely at the mercy of their masters. But free individuals were entitled to governmental protection as the price of their allegiance.

In the 1820s, a leading American legal writer stressed that every person is entitled to "the preventive arm of the magistrate, as a further protection from threatened or impending danger."[2] A number of states had laws making cities and counties liable for damages caused by riots within their jurisdiction, on the theory that they had a duty to prevent the riots from taking place.

When Congress adopted the Fourteenth Amendment, it had every reason to be thinking about the government's duty of protection. Violence against blacks was widespread in the South, met with indifference or knowing acquiescence by state officials. Not surprisingly, the congressional debates are replete with references to the duty to protect, particularly the federal government's duty to protect American citizens. There was a general consensus that, in the words of one congressman, the "first duty of the Government is to afford protection to its citizens."[3]

Of course, as a general matter, the government is not responsible for the actions of private individuals. In lawyers' parlance, they are not "state actors" and therefore not covered by the Fourteenth Amendment. Even the most conscientious government cannot expect to eliminate crimes and other abusive conduct. As everyone agreed, Joshua's father was not a state actor. But this does not answer the question of whether state officials shared some of the responsibility for the harm done to Joshua.

In rejecting Joshua's claims, Chief Justice Rehnquist lumped the right to protection with other affirmative rights to government assistance like welfare payments or public housing. He seemed concerned that a ruling for Joshua could open the door to other possible constitutional claims for government help. The right to protection against private violence, however, is much better established historically than welfare rights and originated long before the idea of the modern welfare state was even hatched.

The Court may also have been worried that recognition of a right to protection would lead federal courts to become deeply involved in the management of state law enforcement. To the extent that resource allocations favor some citizens over others in terms of how much government protection they receive, perhaps some degree of judicial oversight would not be such a bad idea. Don't forget that one of the other clauses of the Fourteenth Amendment guarantees everyone the "equal protection of the laws." This has been construed to be a general ban on discrimination, but the core meaning of this mandate is simply that the government has to protect everyone equally.

However, to have decided in Joshua's favor, no sweeping judicial scrutiny of law enforcement would be necessary. In other settings the Supreme Court has recognized that "deliberate indifference" is different from negligence or being unreasonable. Because of the Supreme Court's ruling, the full facts of the case were never developed at trial. But as described by the Court, the caseworker's actions seem to come very close to deliberate indifference. This should be actionable. It is one thing to fault a police department for assigning cops to the wrong part of town or the wrong kinds of cases, or for failing to hire enough cops in the first place. It is quite another to point a finger at a police officer who sits by for no apparent reason while listening to a victim's screams. Joshua's case is a good deal closer to the latter situation than the former one.

Instead of twisting itself into the decision it had made, the Supreme Court would have done better to remember the Ninth Amendment and the P or I Clause. They stand as reminders of the Constitution's recognition of basic human rights. And none is more basic than the right of a child to government protection against violence.

17

The Right to Travel and Other Rights

The Ninth Amendment by its nature protects a continuum of liberty, not just a few specified rights. The potential breadth of the Amendment is illustrated by some additional examples. First is the right to travel. The Ninth could be used to confirm the right to interstate travel, which the Supreme Court has endorsed but never identified with a particular part of the Constitution. And it could be used to validate the right of Americans to travel abroad, which the Court has never done.

Two other rights are worth further investigation. One is the right to continued possession of one's home. This obviously is not an absolute right, but it may deserve some degree of protection. Until now, the Supreme Court has regarded eviction from one's home as being constitutionally interchangeable with termination of a commercial lease. This may deserve rethinking.

The second possible area for constitutional protection is informational privacy. The Fourth Amendment protects against government seizure of information, but it does not limit disclosure of whatever information the government does lawfully collect. Given rapidly changing technologies, this is an area where courts should tread carefully, but it may make sense for them to play a role.

THE RIGHT TO TRAVEL

The right to travel had roots in earlier decisions but received its most important recognition in a 1969 welfare rights case.[1] Rules in several states and in Washington, D.C., denied welfare assistance to residents who had not resided in the jurisdiction for at least one year. The Court observed that it had "long ago recognized that the nature of our Federal Union and our constitutional concepts of personal liberty unite to require that all citizens be free to travel throughout the length and breadth of our land uninhibited by statutes, rules, or regulations which unreasonably burden or restrict this movement."

The Court also noted in the welfare ruling that its precedents had never settled on a constitutional home for this right. At least three clauses have been invoked at one time or another. Most recently, the Court has referred to the P or I Clause of the Fourteenth Amendment as a partial source of this right. The Ninth Amendment would also bolster this right, particularly to the extent that the federal government rather than Congress might seek to limit it. Federal restrictions on interstate travel for lawful purposes may seem far-fetched, but one can imagine such restrictions coming as part of some overly zealous anti-terrorist program. Clarifying the right to travel across state lines would be useful.

One gap in current law is whether there is also a right to travel within a single state. A dramatic example of this issue came in the aftermath of Hurricane Katrina. Seeking to flee New Orleans, desperate refugees tried to cross the bridge into the town of Gretna. The Gretna police forcibly turned back the refugees and closed the bridge. Since the bridge did not cross state lines, it is unclear whether the refugees had a constitutional right to travel out of New Orleans. Yet it is surely a fundamental deprivation of liberty to be confined to a specific city—this is the sort of restriction we might impose on paroled criminals or defendants out on bail, but not on ordinary citizens. The Ninth Amendment and the P or I Clause would provide a strong basis for a right of intrastate travel. It seems weird to say there is a right to travel from Manhattan to Philadelphia but no right to travel from Houston to Dallas.

Foreign travel is even less established as a constitutional right. The Supreme Court has sometimes required Congress to provide clear guidelines before restricting travel, but it has never held that Congress's power over foreign travel had limits. Thus, on current constitutional understandings, there seems to be no clear barrier to prevent Congress from creating a kind of Berlin Wall, physically blocking people from leaving the country at will. The right to exit is basic in a free society. It is a right that the Ninth Amendment can easily be understood to protect.

The Supreme Court gave some evidence of sensitivity to this right in a Warren Court decision, but the Burger Court backpedaled. In a 1958 case, the Warren Court reversed the government's decision to deny a man a passport because he would not submit an affidavit about Communist Party membership. The Court held that "the right to travel is a part of the 'liberty' of which the citizen cannot be deprived without the due process of law under the Fifth Amendment."

As the Court observed, the right to international travel emerged as early as Magna Charta. Article 42 of Magna Charta reads: "'It shall be lawful to any person, for the future, to go out of our kingdom, and to return, safely and securely, by land or by water, saving his allegiance to us, unless it be in time of war, for some short space, for the common good of the kingdom: excepting prisoners and outlaws, according to the laws of the land, and of the people of the nation at war against us, and Merchants who shall be treated as it is said above." (Similarly, today, the Universal Declaration of Human Rights says that "everyone has the right to leave any country, including his own, and to return to his country.") Thus, the Court said, "freedom of movement across frontiers in either direction, and inside frontiers as well, was a part of our heritage. Travel abroad, like travel within the country, may be necessary for a livelihood. It may be as close to the heart of the individual as the choice of what he eats, or wears, or reads. Freedom of movement is basic in our scheme of values."

For this reason, the Court said, restrictions on freedom of international movement must, at a minimum, be clearly legislated by Congress, not imposed at the discretion of the executive branch: "Since we start with an exercise by an American citizen of an activity included in constitutional protection, we will not readily infer that Congress gave the Secretary of State unbridled discretion to grant or withhold it."

Although the Burger Court gave lip service to this ruling, it eroded the 1958 decision in a case involving a former CIA agent, Philip Agee, who was seeking to expose U.S. covert activities. (In that less enlightened era of our nation's history, it apparently did not occur to the government simply to grab him and ship him to Guantanamo for the rest of his life.) The upshot of the case was to give the government wide power to halt international travel by withdrawing passports in the name of national security.[2]

The Court emphasized that "the *freedom* to travel outside the United States must be distinguished from the *right* to travel within the United States." Although the right to interstate travel is almost completely protected, "the 'right' of international travel has been considered to be no more than an aspect of the 'liberty' protected by the Due Process Clause of the Fifth Amendment. As such this 'right,' the Court has held, can be regulated within the bounds of due process." The Court found that the interest in national security was sufficiently compelling to justify restrictions on travel. Undoubtedly this was true. However, the Court completely distorted past history to trump up a basis for finding that Congress had approved of this alleged presidential authority.

As Justice Brennan's dissent explained, the reasoning used by the Court to establish congressional approval was deeply inconsistent with the reasoning of the 1958 case, which had rejected very similar efforts to justify travel restrictions. Justice Brennan tartly observed that the *Agee* case seemed a prime example of the adage that "bad facts make bad law." He admitted that the former CIA agent "is hardly a model representative of our Nation," and that the executive branch's only hope of stopping his damaging disclosures was to revoke his passport. But, Brennan said, "just as the Constitution protects both popular and unpopular speech, it likewise protects both popular and unpopular travelers." As Brennan said, "it is important to remember that this decision applies not only to Philip Agee, whose activities could be perceived as harming the national security, but also to other citizens who may merely disagree with Government foreign policy and express their views."

The right to international travel has deep historical roots.[3] For example, Queen Elizabeth's charter to settle America authorized the recipient to "inhabite there with him such and soe many of our subjects as shall willingly accompany him." This was in stark contrast to the French and Spanish policies of colonization, which strictly controlled travel to the New World. Similar language was used in the charter for Jamestown, Virginia. In 1641, Massachusetts proclaimed that everyone "shall have free libertie, not with standing any Civill power, to remove both himself and his familie at their pleasure out of the same, provided there be no legall impediment to the contrarie." After the Revolution, the Articles of Confederation granted "free ingress and egress to and from any other state." It was not until 1918 that Congress first limited outward freedom of movement by demanding that citizens leaving the country get passports.

The history of peacetime restrictions on foreign travel by Americans is not a happy one. During the Cold War, permission to travel abroad was denied capriciously. For eight years, the government denied a passport to an expert on radioactive tracers in the body. He wanted to go to Australia for a year as a visiting professor and to attend scientific conferences in France and England. Apparently, he had had dinner with a Soviet vice consul and had been overheard discussing radioactive treatment for an embassy official with leukemia. Because he was considered a possible subversive, the playwright Arthur Miller was denied permission to travel to Brussels to see one of his own plays open. At other times, passports were denied for a dissident congressman who wanted to make a fact-finding visit abroad and for a black war hero who might have criticized U.S. racial policy while abroad. More recently, the government has denied reentry to the United States to citizens suspected (apparently with little articulated basis) of terrorist connections in order to force them to cooperate with investigators. None of this suggests that the government can be safely entrusted with unrestricted power over travel.

The Ninth Amendment provides a solid basis for providing constitutional protection to the right to travel. At the very least, the Court should reaffirm the requirement that Congress provide clear authorization for limits on foreign travel. Given the recent extravagant claims to executive power made by the current administration, there is no reason to expect the executive branch to exercise self-restraint. More than that, however, the Court should make it clear that even Congress does not have unlimited power to regulate foreign travel. Undoubtedly, there are sometimes valid reasons to restrict travel. But the burden should be on the government to demonstrate the existence of such reasons and to show that any restrictions on travel are carefully tailored to their justifications.

THE RIGHT TO POSSESS YOUR HOME

The point of the Ninth Amendment is that no list can be comprehensive. Certainly the one in this book is not. I would like to suggest a couple of other possible candidates for inclusion on the list. Of course, it would take considerable further discussion to determine whether they should really go on the list and, if so, just how they should be defined.

One is the right not to be evicted from one's home without good reason. There are two Supreme Court cases that conflict with this right. In one case, the Supreme Court allowed states to use streamlined eviction procedures on tenants, short-circuiting the right to a full hearing. (The other case, discussed below, involves seizing homes through eminent domain.) Under the Supreme Court's ruling in the eviction case, a tenant who had the legal right to withhold rent under state law would not be allowed to present that claim in the eviction proceeding. Instead, she would have to wait until later, after she was thrown out of her home, to seek some form of redress.

The facts of the case show just how unfair this rule can be. The tenants rented a single-family house in Portland, Oregon. In early November, the City Bureau of Buildings declared the dwelling unfit for habitation. City inspectors found rusted gutters, broken windows, broken plaster, missing rear steps, and improper sanitation. The tenants asked the landlord to make certain repairs, which, with one minor exception, he refused to do. They had paid the November rent but refused to pay the December rent until the repairs had been made.

Under state law, the deck was stacked against them when the landlord decided to evict them for nonpayment of rent rather than make the repairs. Tenants were entitled to only two days' notice before the hearing, with a possible continuance of another two days. They had to post a bond to get a longer continuance or to appeal the case. They also faced the risk of being charged twice the rent if they appealed unsuccessfully (the only part of the statute that the Supreme Court ultimately rejected).

The Court announced that it gave no special constitutional protection to the tenants' rights to keep their home when in fact they did not owe any rent. As the Court explained: "We do not denigrate the importance of decent, safe, and sanitary housing. But the Constitution does not provide judicial remedies for every social and economic ill." Thus, the fact that a residence was involved made no difference: the tenants got the same constitutional protection as the corporate tenant of a commercial lease in the local mall, which is to say no protection at all.

As the dissent pointed out, the upshot of the law was that residential tenants got very little opportunity to present their cases:

> For slum tenants—not to mention the middle class—this kind of summary procedure usually will mean in actuality no opportunity to be heard. Finding a lawyer in two days, acquainting him with the facts, and getting necessary witnesses make the theoretical opportunity to be heard and interpose a defense is a promise of empty words. It is, indeed, a meaningless notice and opportunity to defend. The trial is likely to be held in the presence of only the judge and the landlord and the landlord's attorney.

An important point to note is that the landlord could only collect the overdue rent in a separate action, in which the tenant could raise the defense that the building did not meet code. But even if a tenant won this later action, she would already have been evicted for nonpayment of rent that she didn't actually owe. Of course, all of this puts heavy pressure on tenants to pay their rent even if the building fails to meet code, although they are not legally obligated to do so.

Homeowners have received equally scant protection. In the *Kelo* case, the Supreme Court upheld the use of eminent domain to seize a woman's longtime home for the use of a private development project.[4] The house had been in her family for more than one hundred years. She was born in the house in 1918; her husband, petitioner Charles Dery, moved into the house when they married in 1946. Their son, who also joined the lawsuit, lived next door with his family in the house he was given as a wedding gift. Under existing law the nature of the property made no difference; a vacant lot receives the same protection from eminent domain as a lifelong home. As Justice Thomas pointed out in his dissent, no compensation is provided "for the subjective value of these lands to the individuals displaced and the indignity inflicted by uprooting them from their homes."

The issue before the Court was whether economic redevelopment counted as a public purpose, and the Court said it did. This interpretation of the public use requirements of the Fifth Amendment was supported by precedent and might well have been correct. However, it might be argued that the Court should give a greater degree of protection to homeowners. Of course, there may be occasions when there is no alternative to seizing a private home, whether to build a highway or for urban renewal. Still, we might treat people's homes under the Constitution the way parkland is treated by federal statutes, which prohibit parks from being used for roads unless there is no feasible and prudent alternative. Alternatively, we might at least adjust the compensation award upward to compensate for the blow of being forced out of one's home. A Ninth Amendment right to keep one's home could provide constitutional security for many Americans.

There is some international support for the right to housing. The Universal Declaration of Human Rights declares that everyone has the right to housing. The South African constitution provides that "everyone has the right to have access to adequate housing" and that the state must take "reasonable measures, within its available resources" to achieve this goal. One South African case involved nine hundred people who were being ejected from a squatter settlement and had nowhere else to go. Some had been on waiting lists for government housing for as long as seven years. Their homes were bulldozed and their possessions destroyed. They took shelter under plastic sheeting on a sports field, where they were pelted by driving winter rains. The court held that the government was obligated to create a short-term emergency housing program and a longer-range program to expand the housing supply.

In another case, the court held that an eviction would not be "fair and equitable" unless the squatters had some other place to move their homes. The court also said that judges should be "far more cautious in evicting well-settled families with strong local ties" than recently arrived squatters. But later litigation makes it clear that failing to provide alternative housing violates not only the rights of the squatters but the property rights of the landowner who is unable to conduct the evictions. Hence, the property owner was entitled to government compensation for the continued occupation of his land.[5]

The South African constitutional scheme is different from ours and puts considerable emphasis on social welfare rights. Thus, it would be wrong to argue for simply transferring these results to U.S. law. But the South African cases do provide an interesting alternative model, which may broaden our sense of what options are available in terms of constitutional interpretation.

INFORMATIONAL PRIVACY

Another right that might be considered is that of privacy, in the sense of restrictions on the public disclosure of personal information. In a 1970s case, the Court intimated that there might be some constitutional restrictions on the government's right to disclose private information.[6] A New York law required that prescriptions for certain dangerous drugs be reported to state authorities, but it provided safeguards against public disclosure. The Court found the safeguards to be sufficient but did seem to exhibit some sensitivity to the privacy concerns at issue.

"We are not unaware," wrote Justice Stevens in his majority opinion, "of the threat to privacy implicit in the accumulation of vast amounts of personal information in computerized data banks or other massive government files." Many government functions "require the orderly preservation of great quantities of information, much of which is personal in character and potentially embarrassing or harmful if disclosed." Generally, Stevens observed, the government's right to use and collect the data is accompanied by a duty to avoid unwarranted disclosures. He recognized "that in some circumstances that duty arguably has its roots in the Constitution." However, the state had shown "a proper concern with, and protection of, the individual's interest in privacy." Since the safeguards were sufficient, the Court found it unnecessary to reach the question of whether a constitutional right was truly involved in the case.

Today, computerized databases are far more pervasive and far more invasive of individual privacy than they were thirty years ago. We are all aware of the risks of identity theft and of the threat to individual privacy posed by deliberate or inadvertent disclosure of these caches of information. We may ultimately come to view the right to be protected against such disclosure as truly fundamental to life in a free society. For now, it is unclear whether we have reached that point, but the Supreme Court has at least left the door open for such a ruling. Consequently, there is at least a possible basis for considering such privacy to be a Ninth Amendment right.

An international comparison is again enlightening. The European Convention on Human Rights recognizes a right to respect for private life and personal correspondence. This right has been applied to issues such as phone tapping and the use of medical records in court. If we were to recognize such a right in U.S. constitutional law, it would obviously take considerable thought to define that right in a manageable way. Clearly, we do not want courts supervising the government's choice about software security at a detailed level—as a group, federal judges probably know less about this kind of issue than many fifteen-year-olds. Still, there may be some appropriate role for judicial intervention in extreme cases. As Justice Breyer has recently suggested, it may be useful for courts to take small steps in this area. He suggests that a ruling that explains the Court's concerns without creating a broad rule may be a useful prod for Congress to rewrite the rules as technology progresses.[7]

The Ninth Amendment is, quite literally, about rights without number. It is these unnumbered rights that are to be given the same status as the enumerated ones. I do not claim that it will always be easy to determine which rights rank as fundamental. But over time, if they carefully consider the relevant factors, courts can make reasonable judgments about where to draw the line.

PART FOUR

Broader Implications

18

Fundamental Rights and the Judicial Process

Lochner illustrates the dangers that can arise when courts undertake to pronounce on fundamental values. From the modern perspective, it seems bizarre that the Court would give constitutional status to the "right" of bakers to work more than sixty hours a week. Clearly, judges can make serious mistakes in identifying fundamental rights. Why, then, should we take the risk?

For originalists, the answer depends completely on the historical record. We should take those risks because the Ninth Amendment and the P or I Clause were designed to protect fundamental rights. End of story.

For those who do not limit themselves to the original understanding, the answer is more complex. It seems clear that in the United States, as in many other parts of the world, we have decided that the risks connected with the protection of fundamental rights are worth running. This may stem in part because of what the world learned during World War II about the critical need to protect human rights. The risk of the occasional unnecessary intrusion on political institutions has seemed worth running in order to avoid the opposing risk of human rights violations. In the U.S. system, however, the issue is not seriously in doubt. We have come to rely on the Court to perform this role over many decades. A judicial nominee who explicitly disavowed this role—for example, by arguing in favor of the state's power to ban contraception—would not be confirmable.

The real question is not whether judges should play this role, but how they should do so. In my view, there are guidelines but no formula that can guarantee the correct result. Good constitutional decisions involve neither the mechanical application of formal rules nor the freewheeling ways of pure politics. They rely instead on judgment and discretion, which by definition incorporate both flexibility and constraints.

My approach to interpreting the Ninth Amendment, then, cannot be captured in a catchword or a set of instructions. But that does not mean that judges can simply rule willy-nilly on which rights are fundamental. The history of Anglo-American courts now stretches back almost a thousand years. During that time judges have made and remade the common law, but the process has been evolutionary rather than revolutionary.

Today, the fashion in constitutional theory tends toward sweeping abstractions that purportedly can constrain willful judges from bad decisions. Originalists claim that if judges would only pledge allegiance to the original understanding, all our problems would be solved. Other scholars argue that the secret answer lies in political philosopher John Rawls's writings or in reading the text of the Constitution with the same obsession with detail as that of an English professor reading *Paradise Lost*. Still others believe that the sole goal of the courts should be equal political participation by all citizens. What they all have in common is a belief that the legal system cannot really work without their theories. They find repugnant the kind of case-by-case decision making that state and federal judges use every day.

Much of the discussion about judicial review is distorted by an almost superstitious sense that it is a suspect practice. This attitude leads either to a fear of undemocratic rule by unelected judges or to an effort to tame this fear by making the judges mere puppets of the earlier generations who wrote the Constitution. This attitude seems increasingly anachronistic in a world where judicial review is the rule rather than the exception for democracies. Protection of fundamental rights by courts is far from being suspect. Rather, it is now more the norm than the exception.

The reason for the spread of judicial review is simple: much of the rest of the world has come to share the American view that some basic values are too important to be left entirely to the protection of politicians. Majority rule by itself cannot be completely trusted to protect religious, political, racial, and geographic minorities from oppression. This is a lesson Americans learned early, in the years before the Constitution was drafted. Other countries learned the lesson more recently in the post–World War II wave of protections for human rights.

Once we put aside this obsessive insecurity about the role of judges, we can see that they have been quietly performing their jobs without the help of any of the overarching theories that scholars love so much. If you don't think it is possible to decide cases in a principled way without the benefit of a "Big Think" theory, just watch them. It has been said that at one point aeronautical engineers had proved that it was impossible for bumblebees to fly. Critics today seem to think it is impossible for judges to make reasoned decisions without the benefit of strict legal formulas. But the bumblebees kept on flying, and judges have been engaging in the exercise of reasoned judgment for centuries. If theorists cannot account for these phenomena, so much the worse for their theories.

The fact is that we do not need sweeping theories or completely predictable judges in order for the system to work. We have built a number of safeguards into the judicial system to keep judges from straying too far. The first, of course, is the selection process.

Becoming a federal judge involves a careful screening process. The process doesn't always work, and some presidents may be less reliable than others in their selections. But the process does tend to produce competent, hardworking, honest judges, who truly want to do their jobs well.

We also go to great lengths to imbue judges with a special attitude toward their work. We limit their exposure to outside influences, strictly forbidding discussions with outsiders about pending cases. There are no friendly lobbyists to wine and dine them while they are deciding cases. We also make judges explain the reasons for their decisions, and these explanations are part of the public record. And judges are never completely on their own. Trial judges must answer to higher courts, and appellate judges sit in groups so that no one judge has the final say.

One function of law is social stability, and one appeal of a formulaic approach is its promise of stability. Fortunately, we can have the stability without having the formula, because stability requires only that most cases be reasonably predictable. Because there are easy cases, most of which never reach the Supreme Court, constitutional law can provide a stable framework for government. It is important to note that many cases that would have been quite difficult when a constitutional provision was adopted can later become easy because they are controlled by precedent. So we need not fear that the law will be reduced to chaos if we abandon the quest for the perfect decision-making formula. Many cases will be straightforward, and reasonable judges will readily agree on the outcomes.

This is about the best that any system of decision making can guarantee. A judge in a challenging case is trying to solve a difficult problem. In general, there is no simple recipe for problem solving, whether the problem arises in law, business, engineering, or medicine. We can help prepare people to solve such problems in various ways by giving them basic tools they need to analyze problems, talking in general terms about good ways to approach problems, and exposing them to case studies of similar problems. That is, for example, how business schools train corporate managers and how law schools train future lawyers and judges. But there is an element of creativity in finding solutions that simply cannot be reduced to a formula, and efforts at guidance simply fade into platitudes.

No doubt, it would be wonderful to have some recipe for making difficult decisions. But the absence of such a program is simply part of the human condition. Life presents complex choices. In making these difficult decisions, people expand their knowledge, revise their understanding of who they are, and better grasp their fundamental values. What is true in personal life is also true in constitutional law. The big decisions cannot be reduced to a formula.

This kind of unstructured but still "reasoned" decision making is certainly familiar to American lawyers. Attention to precedent and policy dominates the common law. Many important bodies of American law, including torts, contracts, and property, are controlled by the common law to this day. Others, such as criminal law, are rooted in concepts originally developed by the common law or, like antitrust rules, represent common law elaborations on open-ended statutes.

If you open a random page of the *U.S. Reports* and read one of the Supreme Court's constitutional decisions, you will be struck by how much of the space is devoted to discussing the Court's previous rulings. Indeed, the constitutional text may only be mentioned in a footnote, and discussion of original intent may or may not be present—but discussion of precedent is universal and generally thorough. Some critics decry this reliance on precedent, but whatever one may think about it, it is clearly a key part of judicial practice.

Neither precedent nor principle nor logic alone can dictate results. Judges must often make choices among plausible applications or extensions of existing doctrine. Those choices will be influenced by myriad factors, including the judge's own policy preferences and views of the judicial role, the persuasiveness of the lawyers, the judge's perception of public or legislative sentiment, and so on. These factors might sometimes counsel restraint and sometimes not. But one factor that influences judges always serves as a brake rather than as a goad: a preference for evolutionary rather than radical change.

The abortion issue illustrates how this evolutionary process can operate. It is true that *Roe* was a big step—probably too big a step— but it grew out of earlier decisions establishing a right to contraception and standing more generally for a right of procreative freedom. *Roe* itself erred by trying to lay down, once and for all, a set of comprehensive rules governing the exercise of the abortion right. But a series of later cases gradually hammered away at these rules as new statutes were passed, refining the rules into a kind of reasonableness test. The Court made its embrace of that test explicit in *Casey*, and the law will no doubt continue to evolve in later cases.

As Justice Souter has explained, this kind of evolutionary process is basic to the common law. As he puts it, the "usual thinking of the common law is suspicion of the all-or-nothing analysis that tends to produce legal petrification instead of an evolving boundary between the domains of old principles." Thus, common law reasoning seeks to "understand old principles afresh by new examples and new counterexamples." The result, he said, is a living tradition, "albeit one that moves by moderate steps carefully taken."[1]

The judiciary is, by nature and by design, the most conservative part of the government. The judiciary's task is to look back on past traditions and simultaneously preserve them and update them to meet the challenges of the present and the future. Radical or revolutionary reform is inconsistent with this role. In common law adjudication, the law usually changes slowly, through accretion and subtle revision of precedents rather than through sudden or fundamental shifts in policy. Constitutional adjudication is similarly constrained.

In praising the evolutionary nature of the law, I do not mean that the Supreme Court should only take "baby steps." What is important is not the size of the individual step, but the fact that each is understood to be only one in a series of steps through which the Court works out its path. Just as the common law evolves in a series of decisions, constitutional law is most successful when the Court is able to develop principles over a sustained series of cases rather than trying to emulate a legislature by pronouncing a binding set of rules all at once.

In the context of Ninth Amendment rights, the common law system ensures that the law will retain stability because of respect for precedent. At the same time, the common law has always had a capacity to grow and respond to a changing world.

As I have tried to show, courts are not entirely left at large when trying to define fundamental rights. Although there is no easy formula for deciding cases, there are some important guidelines. One of these, to which I have referred frequently, is what the drafters of the Declaration of Independence called a decent respect for the opinions of humankind. This openness to considering the views of others outside of our borders is perhaps the most controversial aspect of my proposed guidelines. I have already touched on this issue, giving some preliminary justifications for consulting non-U.S. law in fundamental rights cases. It is time, however, for a more extended treatment of the subject.

19

Joining the Rest of the World

The Framers of the Constitution were no isolationists. They were immersed in legal thinking from around the world. In turn, they brought this learning to bear when they wrote the Ninth Amendment and its Fourteenth Amendment cousin. Too many of those who claim to worship them and their work, however, want to build a wall between U.S. constitutional law and the rest of the world. The Framers had the better of this disagreement with their self-appointed disciples. Given the amount of heat that surrounds this issue, it is clearly worth a closer look.

THE DEBATE OVER CITATION OF FOREIGN LAW

None other than the late Chief Justice William Rehnquist once explained why increasing reliance on foreign law is a natural development, though he waffled on the issue later. As Rehnquist explained, for "nearly a century and a half, courts in the United States exercising the power of judicial review had no precedents to look to save their own, because our courts alone exercised this kind of authority."

Today, however, "now that constitutional law is firmly grounded in so many countries, it is time that the United States courts begin looking to the decisions of other constitutional courts to aid in their own deliberative process." He called U.S. courts laggard in this respect, but predicted that "with so many thriving constitutional courts in the world today . . . that approach will be changed in the near future."[1]

More recently, in considering the scope of the constitutional prohibition on cruel and unusual punishment, Justices Kennedy and O'Connor both spoke of the significance of international rulings, though they disagreed about the proper outcome of the case.[2] Justice Kennedy, writing for the majority, said that the "opinion of the world community, while not controlling our outcome, does provide respected and significant confirmation for our own conclusions." In dissent, Justice O'Connor explained that America's "evolving understanding of human dignity certainly is neither wholly isolated from, nor inherently at odds with, the values prevailing in other countries." On the contrary, she said, "we should not be surprised to find congruence between domestic and international values, especially where the international community has reached clear agreement— expressed in international law or in the domestic law of individual countries—that a particular form of punishment is inconsistent with fundamental human rights."

This is a sound view of the relationship between U.S. constitutional law and foreign law. It especially behooves us to learn from other constitutional schemes, because many of them (as well as parts of international human rights schemes) were modeled on our own. As Judge Guido Calabresi says, wise parents learn from their children.[3] This is also true of international human rights law. Modern human rights law began with the Nuremberg Charter, the United Nations Charter, and the United Nations Organization—all of them initiatives of the United States. The upshot was the U.N.'s 1948 Universal Declaration of Human Rights. Its premises are much like those of our own Declaration of Independence. The Universal Declaration proclaims that "all human beings are born free and equal in dignity and rights" and that "everyone has the right to life, liberty, and security of person."

It particularly makes sense to go beyond domestic law in identifying and applying Ninth Amendment rights. Madison and his colleagues (as well as the later John Bingham in drafting the Fourteenth Amendment) believed they were protecting the rights of humanity, not some peculiarly American hang-ups about government conduct.

Conservatives have responded with near hysteria to the idea of relying on foreign law. In 2004 and 2005, Senate and House Republicans introduced resolutions banning the use of foreign legal authorities. Representative Sensenbrenner warned that American sovereignty was at risk. Another Republican congressman bemoaned the use of English authority in particular. After all, patriots had "spilled their blood . . . to sever ties with England forever"—what could be worse than "justice in this land of America" using British court decisions in interpreting *our* Constitution? What the British "could not accomplish by force," he trumpeted, "our Supreme Court has surrendered to them voluntarily." A House member named Tom Feeney proposed a bill that would make citation of foreign law an impeachable offense.

Outside of Congress, the response was even wilder. There was the demand that Justice Kennedy be impeached because citing foreign law "upholds Marxist-Leninist, satanic principles." Another impeachment call came from the head of a home-schooling group. Going even further, a self-proclaimed "patriotic" Web site—apparently that term really is sometimes the last refuge of scoundrels— called for the assassination of Justices Ginsburg and O'Connor for having "publicly stated that they use European law and rulings to decide how to rule on American cases."

Some of the resistance seems to be based on a xenophobic disdain for anything foreign, as if only U.S. law can be taken seriously.

Perhaps this xenophobia is not too surprising, given other indica-
tions of national disregard for foreigners. It is remarkable that one
chamber of the national legislature has only recently decided that it
is okay for its food service to go back to using the term "french
fries" instead of calling them "freedom fries." Heaven forbid that
our courts should cite any provisions of French law!

This disdain for whatever is not "American made" doesn't just
come from the lunatic fringe who think the House of Lords is a satanic cult. Justice Thomas refers to "foreign moods, fads, or fashions" when he speaks of non-U.S. law.[4] Justice Scalia sees foreign law
as only a fit subject for idle browsing: "I mean, go ahead and indulge
your curiosity! Just don't put it in your opinions!" Apparently reading foreign law is more or less the equivalent of channel surfing. In
his confirmation hearings, Chief Justice Roberts said: "Foreign law,
you can find anything you want. If you don't find it in the decisions
of France or Italy, it's in the decisions of Somalia or Japan or In-
donesia or whatever." Those wacky foreigners, apparently, will say
just about anything in a judicial opinion.

THE ARGUMENTS AGAINST CITING FOREIGN LAW (AND WHY THEY'RE WRONG)

Although some resistance to consulting foreign law may reflect only
prejudice, there are also some substantive arguments to be considered. One argument is that using foreign law to interpret our Constitution somehow undermines our sovereignty. To some extent,
this argument seems to be based on a simple logical error. The assumption seems to be that if the courts consider legal materials
from outside their jurisdiction, they are giving away their authority
to those other jurisdictions.

That argument, frankly, is ridiculous. State courts cite decisions
from other states constantly, especially nearby states. When a

Nevada court cites California law, it isn't giving the California courts any jurisdiction over Nevada. Such cross-state citations are very common in decisions interpreting state constitutions. One study suggests that more than a third of state constitutional decisions refer to out-of-state cases. In fact, state courts have sometimes specifically suggested that lawyers discuss the relevance of out-of-state rulings. Are we supposed to believe that using California rulings to interpret the Nevada constitution somehow makes Nevada a colony of California?

Another argument is that the U.S. Constitution is purely based on our own culture and history. Hence, there is supposedly nothing we can learn about it from outsiders. For example, Justice Scalia says that he does not believe that "approval by 'other nations and peoples' should buttress our commitment to American principles any more than (what should logically follow) disapproval by 'other nations and peoples' should weaken that commitment." The crux of the argument is that American constitutional guarantees, such as free speech or due process or the ban on slavery, represent distinctively *American* principles, *not* universal principles of human rights. This is just wrong historically, in terms of the original understanding that Justice Scalia claims to be so fond of.

Justice Scalia has also been known to castigate others for failing to pay sufficiently close attention to the text of the Constitution. There's actually a bit of text that speaks to the reasons for protecting rights. The Bill of Rights, by and large, simply presents rights without explaining the reasons. However, there is an exception: the Second Amendment. Here's what the Second Amendment says: "A well-ordered militia, *being necessary to the security of a free State*, the right of the people to keep and bear Arms, shall not be abridged." This is the one place where the Constitution explains its own rationale for protecting a right.

That rationale is something that not everyone would agree with today, but what is clear is that the Second Amendment does not purport to be based on an "American principle." The Second Amendment could have said, "a well-ordered militia being necessary to our security," or "a well-ordered militia being a principle of American government." Instead, it claims to derive from a universal truth about what is necessary for a free society. I don't want to enter the thicket of the gun control debate here. The point I am making is simply that the one time the Framers chose to speak about their reason for protecting rights in the Constitution itself, they invoked what they considered to be a universal principle rather than anything specific to the United States.

There is a deeper issue here: the nature of our own Constitution. A number of critics of foreign law—mostly but not entirely from the Right—argue that foreign constitutionalism is based on a different theory from the one held by Americans. Our Constitution, supposedly, gains all of its strength from the populist act of ratification. Its contents are the dictates of "We the People." What makes the Constitution important is that it is the law we have given ourselves. In contrast, foreign constitutions are based on the idea that people have universal human rights, which should be honored apart from any peculiar mandates of local law.

This argument misunderstands both the intellectual perspectives and moral aspirations of those who gave us the Bill of Rights and the later amendments. When the Constitution was framed and when the post–Civil War amendments were adopted, the law of nations was well understood to be the background for U.S. law. And those who came forth with our constitutional guarantees of rights had the same view. They did not think that rights were merely an outgrowth of local culture or existed only when some legal document gave them official recognition.

The supporters of the Thirteenth Amendment believed that slavery was a universal wrong, not just a violation of some peculiarly American norm. If anything, the reverse was true: the United States was unique among Western societies in allowing slavery; owning slaves could almost be said to be as American as apple pie. When they sought to protect basic rights in the Fourteenth Amendment such as freedom of speech, the same legislators were keenly aware that those rights had often been violated in Southern states and sometimes in the North.

Earlier, during the Ninth Amendment period, judicial opinions, state constitutional provisions, and pronouncements by statesmen made it clear that rights stemmed from a greater source than any local charter or constitution. Don't forget the Declaration of Independence. It said that people were endowed by their creator with certain inalienable rights; it did not say, "as Britons, we are endowed by English common law and statute with certain rights." Of course, the colonists thought the second part was true too, and they thought to a large extent the rights of English people were a practical codification of the rights of humankind. But at a deep level of principle, they thought rights were not merely creatures of local law.

This is not to say, however, that the use of foreign legal materials is completely unproblematic. Those materials need to be used with care. Some of the more thoughtful critics point to some of the difficulties of assessing foreign legal materials. Clearly, the less familiar the foreign legal system, the more trouble we are likely to have in assessing its meaning. Countries that share much of our legal tradition, like England and Canada, will be the easiest to assess. Societies quite different from ours, such as India or South Africa, may have something to teach us, but we need to keep in mind that there are real differences in their situations. Judges are inevitably going to be more at home with domestic sources of law. All of this is a reason to be *careful*, not a reason to ignore potentially useful insights from other legal systems.

Allied to the difficulty of assessing foreign materials is the need to determine how much weight to give them. Essentially, the closer a foreign jurisdiction is to the United States in terms of historical connections, constitutional provisions, and legal institutions, the more relevant that jurisdiction's decisions. Obviously, foreign law is also entitled to more weight when it is persuasively argued and less weight when it seems to reflect another country's peculiarities. For example, some countries have a single dominant religion tightly integrated into their political and legal systems. To the extent that legal rulings rest on the sectarian views of such a religion, they are less relevant to our more pluralistic society, especially given our constitutional prohibition on the establishment of religion. For this reason, the almost total ban on abortions in Ireland may not tell us very much about how we should interpret our own law.

Jeremy Waldron, a prominent legal philosopher,[5] asks us to consider how we would expect our public health authorities to respond to a new disease threat. "It would be ridiculous to say that because this problem had arisen in the United States, we should look only to American science to solve it." On the contrary, we would try to learn as much as we could from the work of scientists around the world. The same, he says, is true for tough constitutional problems such as the scope of the concept of "cruel and unusual punishment," as applied to questions such as the execution of juveniles. These are tough issues, not easy to think through. By seeing what jurists in other parts of the world have to say, we treat such issues as problems to be solved through reason and through "the enterprise, which many legal systems share, of grappling with, untangling, and resolving the rival rights and claims that come together in issues of this kind."

This is certainly not controversial in other areas of the law. For example, the law of torts (recovery of damages for accidents) even today is largely based on judicial decisions rather than statutes. There are many tough issues in tort law—for example, when the result of an accident is so unforeseeable that the defendant should not be held responsible. Some of the leading cases that deal with this issue are English. It would be laughable for an American judge to write off the reasoning of these cases as un-American and therefore as unworthy of serious consideration.

There are also more specific reasons to attend to foreign decisions. Some constitutional rights, like the limits on search and
seizure, use a standard of reasonableness. Seeing what other democracies do can give us a better sense of reasonableness. Constitutional decisions may also depend on some sense of what is
necessary. For example, if the government says that it is necessary
to restrict travel in order to fight terrorism, it would be useful to
know whether other countries with experience in anti-terrorism
measures share the same view.

In addition, when deciding whether to recognize a right, judges
often consider whether the right can be given a reasonably clear definition and whether the judiciary can provide an effective remedy
for violations of the right. Looking at foreign experience can be
helpful in addressing both those concerns. For example, in the last
chapter I suggested that the Ninth Amendment might encompass a
right to keep your home. In deciding whether to accept this right, it
is useful to know whether other jurisdictions recognize this right
and, if so, how they define it and whether courts have been able to
devise workable remedies.

Or let me give an example that may be more congenial to conservatives. The U.S. Supreme Court has withdrawn almost entirely
from reviewing constitutional issues relating to economic regulation. In the *Lochner* era, it reviewed these regulations intensively to
determine if they were reasonable. Since 1937, the Court has simply
dropped out of this enterprise completely. One reason has been a
fear that there is no principled way to distinguish between valid and
invalid regulations, making the decisions inherently political. In this
regard, it might be instructive to look at foreign decisions that have
tried to draw such lines.

For instance, the German Basic Law recognizes a right of occupational freedom, giving all Germans the right to freely choose their occupation. This is a somewhat appealing notion. But before considering
whether to embrace this right, it would be helpful to know more

about the German experience. Have the Germans managed to define the boundary of this right in a principled way? Has the right played a useful role in German law? Has it left reasonable space for government regulation? Clearly, the answers to these questions don't dictate whether this right should be considered part of our own constitutional order, but they do help address some relevant concerns.

In this instance, it gives me some pause that the German courts have extended constitutional protection to the right to make chocolate-covered puffed rice. (The legislature banned the sale of products that might be confused with chocolate candies; the courts thought a simple warning would be good enough.) The question of how best to eliminate consumer confusion does not strike me as being much within a judge's expertise, and it is also hard for me to see a fundamental human right at stake. Of course, deeper research into the law of Germany and other countries might help assuage some of these concerns. (Or maybe not, if a 1990 summary of the German cases provides a fair picture of the law today.[6]) Still, the German chocolate candy case does seem to provide some support for our own Supreme Court's reluctance to get involved in these disputes.

Whatever you think of the arguments pro and con foreign law, one thing is clear. Citing foreign law is an American tradition that goes back to the first days of the Republic. The ones who want to end this practice are the radicals here—providing another confirmation of Cass Sunstein's description of Justice Scalia and company as "radicals in black robes."

SETTING THE RECORD STRAIGHT ON SUPREME COURT USE OF FOREIGN LAW

Steve Calabresi, a well-known constitutional scholar at Northwestern Law School and the cofounder of the Federalist Society, has coauthored a 164-page law review article that surveys the Supreme Court's use of foreign authority since 1793.[7] The length of the article by itself may tell you everything you need to know: there have been a lot of Supreme Court opinions citing foreign authority. Here is what the research found, in the authors' own words: "Those political and journalistic commentators who say that the Court has never before cited or relied upon foreign law are clearly and demonstrably wrong. In fact, the Court has relied on such sources to some extent throughout its history." Indeed, early judges felt comfortable enough with foreign sources to quote extensively from Grotius (the great Dutch master of international law) *in Latin* without providing an English translation. (Apparently they hadn't heard of the English Only movement.) In particular, the survey showed that in construing the law of nations, the early Supreme Court considered a variety of foreign sources: the laws and practices of other nations, especially those on the European continent; the views of foreign scholars; and rulings by the English courts. Given the roots of the Ninth Amendment and the Privileges or Immunities Clause in the law of nations, this is a particularly significant finding.

One striking early case to use foreign law was *Brown v. United States*,[8] an outgrowth of the War of 1812. What makes this case so notable is that the Court used foreign law to help interpret a clause in the U.S. Constitution. The question was whether British property had automatically forfeited to the U.S. government when war was declared, giving the president the power to seize the property without any further congressional authorization. Chief Justice Marshall ruled that the answer was no. Marshall said that the Constitution "was framed at a time when this rule . . . was received throughout the civilized world. In expounding that constitution, a construction ought not lightly to be admitted which would give to a declaration of war an effect in this country it does not possess elsewhere." Hence, Marshall concluded, the property did not automatically revert to the

U.S. government, so the president lacked the constitutional power to seize the property without congressional authorization.

Another important use of foreign law came in the dissents from *Dred Scott*, the Supreme Court's infamous proslavery opinion. The dissenters cited English cases as well as European civil law to support their critique of the Court. One of them concluded that the majority opinion conflicted with "fundamental principles of private international law." Notably, Chief Justice Taney took the opposite tack in his opinion, declaring that blacks had no rights that whites are obliged to respect. This is what he said: "No one, we presume, supposes that any change in public opinion or feeling . . . in the civilized nations of Europe or in this country, should induce [this Court] to give to the words of the Constitution a more liberal construction . . . than they were intended to bear when the instrument was framed and adopted."

The Supreme Court also looked to foreign law in one of its early opinions construing the Fourteenth Amendment. In an 1884 case, the issue was whether due process allowed criminal prosecutions to go forward without a grand jury indictment. The Court looked to foreign law to help answer this question. The Constitution, the Court said, was "made for an undefined and expanding future, and for a people gathered and to be gathered from many nations and many tongues." The Court added that "there is nothing in Magna Charta, broadly construed, which ought exclude the best ideas of all systems and of every age." It was, the Court said, "the characteristic principle of the common law to draw its inspiration from every fountain of justice," and we cannot assume "that the sources of its supply have been exhausted."

In the same year, in upholding the federal government's power to issue paper money, the Supreme Court relied on foreign law to show that this power was universally viewed as an inherent power of sovereignty. The Court referred to the common practice of European governments to issue such money, and it also cited a recent English ruling involving the king of Hungary that recognized this power.

It is tempting to continue, but one 164-page survey is enough. The conclusion is clear enough. It is completely legitimate for the Supreme Court to look abroad when interpreting our Constitution. The evidence is particularly strong in this regard for cases involving the law of nations, which is the foundation of our constitutional guarantees for unenumerated rights. Anyone who says otherwise hasn't looked at the evidence.

It is important to be clear on what is at stake here. I am not saying— and as far as I know, nobody else is saying—that foreign law is *binding* on the Supreme Court's interpretation of the Constitution. What I *am* saying is that foreign law often addresses the same fundamental issues that arise under our Constitution. This is particularly true of provisions like the Ninth Amendment that were founded on universalistic concerns rather than on the special nature of our federal system or our doctrine of separation of powers. When other capable people are struggling earnestly with the same issues that concern us, it is foolish to ignore their efforts.

20

The Ninth Amendment and the Future

The message of the Ninth Amendment is all the more important today, when the Supreme Court's protection of human rights is under such violent attack. The story of the Ninth—its roots in American views of natural law; its intent to preserve unenumerated rights; its heir, the Fourteenth Amendment—is more relevant today than ever. It also resonates, in a way that has been completely overlooked, with the emergence of human rights as a powerful concept globally.

History is never free from ambiguity and complexity, and certainty is correspondingly rare in historical inquiry. We cannot be sure precisely what vision of human rights was embraced by the framers of the Ninth Amendment. What we can be fairly sure about, however, is that their views did not correspond with those of Justice Scalia and other current conservatives. The architects of our constitutional system did not see human rights as a limited list of specifics tacked on at the end of the Constitution. Instead, they saw those specifics as exemplifying broader moral principles, which courts were mandated to defend.

The Framers of the U.S. Constitution were at the forefront of this quest in their own time, and the U.S. Supreme Court has often been a source of guidance for others around the world. If we regain the vision of the Framers of the Ninth Amendment today, we can continue to lead the world in human rights.

For years, conservatives have tried to present us with a stark choice: either limit constitutional rights to the specific language of the Bill of Rights (as that language was understood in 1790), or give judges an open license to impose their values on society. The Ninth Amendment tells us, in so many words, that the first choice is wrong and that we need not embrace the second. Instead, we can opt for the responsible development of a body of law protecting "the rights retained by the people."

Applying the Ninth to existing law would certainly lead to some changes, mostly incremental rather than drastic. It would not read into the Constitution every liberal goal any more than it would adopt every conservative goal. It certainly would not read into the Constitution all of my own policy preferences. I personally support some of the policies that I have rejected here as fundamental rights, and I didn't even bother discussing other policies I favor because the argument for calling them fundamental was too tenuous.

The Ninth's greatest promise is not to create anyone's idea of a utopian society but to shift the terms of debate. Instead of hurling slogans at one another about judicial activism, we would have to accept as a fundamental premise of our legal system the Constitution's protection of the essential components of human liberty. We would have to openly take into account legal developments around the world. Then, and only then, would we be able to begin the work of truly defining and protecting the core freedoms the Framers sought to enshrine in the fabric of American life.

I have called for considering a series of factors in determining whether a right qualifies as fundamental. One factor refers to decisions by international lawmakers and judges recognizing the right. I have discussed this at length because it is controversial, not because it is the dominant consideration. The list also includes six factors specifically focusing on our own law and history: (1) Supreme Court precedent establishing the right or analogous rights; (2) connections with specific constitutional guarantees; (3) long-standing, specific traditions upholding the right; (4) contemporary societal consensus about the validity of the right; (5) decisions by American lawmakers and judges recognizing the right; and finally, (6) broader or more recent American traditions consistent with the right. Often, these factors will point in the same direction, just because various decision makers share common historical and social settings or are influenced by each other's opinions. Sometimes, only some of the factors will be present, making a decision more difficult. At best, this checklist falls short of being a formula for resolving all disputes over fundamental rights. What it can do is offer guidance to judges on how to think about the issue.

To a large extent Supreme Court Justices are already engaging in this kind of decision making, and in fact they have been doing so for years. The trouble is that these judges are on the defensive. The legitimacy of their enterprise is under attack. Lacking knowledge of the historical foundations of what they are doing, they have given ineffectual responses. And the lack of this historical understanding has also hindered their ability to formulate their approach clearly.

It is time to stop apologizing for the Court's valiant efforts to "preserve the Blessings of Liberty" (the words of the Constitution itself). Americans should embrace their heritage of support for human rights and join the rest of the world in the effort to articulate those rights.

This does not mean government by Plato's philosopher kings, who will foist their own moral views on the rest of us. Judges should be very much guided by American traditions as well as emerging legislative trends. They should take careful account of the rulings of other judges, here and in other modern democracies.

They should also move slowly most of the time, allowing the political process time to debate the issues. Judges need to be on guard to be sure that their rulings are not based on personal idiosyncrasies, sectarian doctrines, or political ideology. They should be wary of getting too far "ahead of the curve," lest their decisions lose touch with the main body of the law.

Admittedly, regardless of precautions, there is always a risk of error. Courts may slip up, prematurely short-circuiting the political process. But this is simply the cost we pay for having a system of law in place to guard the inalienable rights that Thomas Jefferson and his generation fought to so hard to defend.

It is sometimes said that those who forget history are doomed to repeat it. In this case, however, it is more likely that those who forget history will lose their grasp of their own traditions. Protecting fundamental rights is one of the great American traditions. This tradition stretches from the Declaration of Independence to Madison's framing of the Ninth Amendment, from the creation of the Fourteenth Amendment to the Supreme Court's modern case law. Around the world, others are following in our footsteps. It would be a shame if we forgot this vital aspect of our heritage.

Appendix: Misunderstanding the Framers

Conservatives have produced some ingenious, if implausible, interpretations in an effort to avoid the plain meaning of the Ninth Amendment. One qualm about originalism is that historical evidence usually isn't powerful enough to overcome preexisting preferences about constitutional interpretation. The response of many conservatives to the Ninth Amendment seems to confirm this. Conservative attitudes toward the Amendment fly in the face of the historical record. And yet these same conservatives claim to be originalists, relying on much more ambiguous historical evidence to "prove" that the New Deal was unconstitutional or that the president has a vast reservoir of unchecked power.

The evidence about the meaning of the Ninth Amendment is as clear as you can find in searching the historical record for constitutional meaning. That isn't to say that it is utterly unambiguous or that I claim to have proved my case beyond any reasonable doubt. But if that were the standard, historical evidence could never be used to shed light on constitutional meaning. Proof beyond a reasonable doubt is rarely within a historian's powers.

The arguments for ignoring or minimizing the Ninth Amendment tend to be rather convoluted, like a tax lawyer's argument for a subtle loophole. After all, the point of the conservative argument is that the Amendment means something other than what its words *seem* to say. This takes some fancy footwork. Hence, it takes some careful analysis to identify the flaws in each of the arguments.

Thus, the basic structure of this Appendix is to present some convoluted misreadings of the Ninth Amendment followed by a rebuttal based on careful analysis of the historical documents. This probably does not make for gripping reading, but as a scholar I feel compelled to address competing theories rather than merely give my own interpretations.

As we will see, the conservative interpretations have serious flaws. They do not sit well with the actual language of the Ninth Amendment. They often ignore the clues that Madison gave about exactly where he saw the Ninth Amendment as fitting into the constitutional scheme. They also tend to imply that Congress used the Ninth Amendment to convey some message, when that same message would have been much more clearly conveyed by other proposed constitutional language that was rejected by Congress.

In short, rather than treating the Ninth Amendment as a straightforward statement about inherent individual rights, they seek to make it a cryptic statement about some other subject. In the process, they seem to be engaging in an exercise in cryptography rather than interpretation. The Constitution is not the "da Vinci code," and we should reject arguments for attributing hidden meanings to plain language.

Not an Effort to Preserve State Governmental Power

Conservatives sometimes argue that the Ninth Amendment was designed to preserve states' rights by limiting the power of the federal government. Even without knowing anything about the history, this seems highly unlikely. The Tenth Amendment, by preserving the retained powers of the states, already performs that function; thus, this conservative interpretation makes the Ninth Amendment completely superfluous.

The history confirms what the text itself makes clear: the Ninth Amendment is about individual rights rather than being about the scope of federal powers. Besides the language that became the Ninth Amendment, Madison's proposal had contained a separate precursor of the Tenth Amendment. Not only did this proto–Tenth Amendment deal squarely with the subject of federalism, but Madison clearly did not see it as a twin of the future Ninth Amendment. He discussed it in a separate section of his remarks, and he saw it as fitting into a completely different part of the Constitution.

By trying to turn the Ninth Amendment into a federalism provision, conservatives are simply jumbling Madison's careful choice of language. The federalism argument is made even less appealing by the fact that when new states were admitted to the Union in the nineteenth century, they typically included a version of the Ninth Amendment in their state constitutions. Obviously, they saw the principle of the Ninth Amendment as applying to state governments, not merely as a special kind of protection against the federal government.[1]

NOT AN EFFORT TO PREVENT BACKDOOR EXPANSION OF FEDERAL AUTHORITY

A related argument is that the Ninth Amendment was designed only to prevent a certain, very specific misinterpretation of the Bill of Rights. The misinterpretation itself is based on a chain of reasoning so twisty that only a lawyer could love it. It is a tribute to the ingenuity of the Framers that they identified this argument and thought it was worth debating. What is clear, however, is that this concern was not the basis for the Ninth Amendment.

This argument is based on a very specific claim used to rebut the desirability of a bill of rights: expressly protecting rights can be twisted into an argument for expanding government power in other settings.

As an example of how this argument works, consider the First Amendment's ban on regulations infringing on the free exercise of religion. By including this ban the Bill of Rights could be said to imply that otherwise, if it were *not* for the First Amendment, Congress *would* have power to regulate religion. (Otherwise the First Amendment would not be needed.) Hence, one of Congress's enumerated powers must have been broad enough to regulate religion. If so, that same power must have been broad enough to allow Congress to regulate similar, nonreligious groups such as social clubs. Thus, through a somewhat convoluted legal argument, the existence of a ban on regulating religion could be twisted into an argument for Congress's power to regulate social clubs. Via this backdoor reasoning, the Free Exercise Clause could actually have the effect of expanding the interpretation of federal power beyond what it would otherwise have been.

In Federalist Paper 84, Alexander Hamilton had argued against the desirability of a bill of rights on this ground. He contended that a provision on infringing freedom of the press could be taken to imply that Congress had the power to pass other kinds of regulations of the press, so long as they did not constitute infringements on a free press. In short, an amendment purporting to protect the press could actually backfire and increase other congressional powers, when it otherwise would have been clear that none of these powers really authorized regulation of the press. Thus, a bill of rights would "contain various exceptions to powers which are not granted; and, on this very account, would afford a colorable pretext to claim more than were granted." In a nutshell, this is the argument that a Bill of Rights could be misused to imply that Congress's powers were broader than they really were.

We can be confident that the Ninth Amendment, in the form it was actually adopted, was *not* addressed to this concern. Madison's initial version actually *had* responded to this concern. His draft included language directing that the Bill of Rights "shall not be so construed . . . *to enlarge the powers delegated by the Constitution.*" But that language was dropped from the final version of the Amendment. So this theory requires us to say that Congress had only a single problem in mind but then mysteriously dropped the only explicit language dealing with that problem. Not very likely.

NOT DESIGNED TO PROTECT THE REPEAL OF STATES' BILLS OF RIGHTS

Another conservative argument is that the Ninth Amendment was included only to safeguard *state* constitutional provisions against being repealed by the federal Bill of Rights. The fear, supposedly, was that if a state included an additional safeguard against abuses by its own state government, that safeguard might somehow be nullified by the passage of the federal Bill of Rights. Under this theory, the Ninth Amendment was designed as a countermeasure against another fairly convoluted misinterpretation of the Bill of Rights.

For example, suppose a state constitution went beyond the federal Constitution by prohibiting all laws relating in any way to religion, not just those impairing free exercise or establishing a religion. Since the federal Constitution defined religious freedom more narrowly than the state constitution and since the federal Constitution is the "supreme law of the land," then arguably the state constitution would be invalid for trying to provide broader protection. In other words, somehow adding restrictions on the federal government might be twisted into an argument for wiping out existing state constitutional restrictions on their own governments.

It is utterly mysterious why anyone would have thought that this danger existed in the first place. If a state had placed restrictions on its own government, why would those restrictions be changed by a federal provision placing *other* restrictions on the *federal* government? You might as well argue that by providing a procedure for electing the president, the Constitution was wiping out existing state constitutional provisions for electing state governors. Why would the existence of one provision limiting the federal government repeal another provision in a different document limiting a state government?

It might seem odd to suppose that the Framers added specific language to the Constitution in order to block an argument that itself seems far-fetched if not a bit incomprehensible. But this is one of the theories propounded by conservatives—that basically the Ninth Amendment is merely intended to give states the power to protect additional rights from state legislation in their own constitutions.

A careful reading of Madison's speech on the Bill of Rights shows that he had no such far-fetched danger in mind. Instead, the language conservatives cite was directed to another issue entirely. Madison was responding to one of the other arguments previously made against adopting a federal bill of rights. This argument held that a federal bill of rights was unnecessary because Congress was indirectly bound by the bills of rights in state constitutions. Since the states already had their own bills of rights when they adopted the Constitution, those restrictions might carry over against the federal government as well. This is not an argument that a modern constitutional lawyer would find appealing, so the fact that Madison gives it any credence is of historical interest. However, his consideration of this argument had nothing to do with the Ninth Amendment.

In discussing this point, Madison is describing an argument against the need for a federal bill of rights, an argument that he obviously does not accept since he is now proposing such a bill of rights. Madison rejected this claim that a state constitution's bill of rights could be relied on to limit the federal government. First, he said, this argument was too uncertain to rely on as a protection of liberty from federal interference. It might be accepted, or it might not. And besides, he observed, some states had no bills of rights, while other states' bills of rights defined liberty too restrictively. Thus, counting on state constitutions to restrain the federal government was at best a gamble and certainly not a safe substitute for a federal bill of rights.

The key point is that Madison is not making the case for the Ninth Amendment at this point. Rather, Madison's discussion is intended to show that the Constitution *does* need a Bill of Rights. Trying to piggyback federal rights on state constitutional provisions simply would not work.

Only after disposing of this argument against having a bill of rights does Madison turn to the claim that listing some rights might be read to authorize federal violations of others. He refers to this claim as having *also* been raised—the "also" of course applying that this was a separate claim, not part of the earlier argument against the Bill of Rights based on the existence of state constitutional rights. Contrary to the view of some commentators, he is obviously changing the subject, not continuing his description of state constitutional rights. As is too often the case, in lumping these points together, originalists are surprisingly sloppy in their treatment of the historical record.

OTHER MISINTERPRETATIONS: COLLECTIVE RIGHTS AND UNBOUNDED LIBERTIES

Another effort to dodge the Ninth Amendment holds that it refers only to collective rights such as the right to redo the scheme of government through a constitutional convention. This reading might make more sense if the Ninth Amendment had been proposed by the opponents of the Constitution, who were worried about the effect of the Constitution on self-government, among other possible risks. But unlike the other Amendments, the Ninth was the product of Madison's own initiative, not that of the skeptics who had been worried about adopting the Constitution.

This theory simply does not fit with what we know about Madison and his concerns at the time. There is no reason to suspect that Madison himself had ever worried about the effect of a Bill of Rights on the right to call a constitutional convention. If he had been, presumably he would have proposed adding the Ninth Amendment to Article V of the Constitution, which covers constitutional conventions and other amendment procedures, rather than in connection with limitations on the power of Congress. Or if he had been worried about self-government more generally, he might have tried placing it together with the Constitution's guarantee of a "republican form of government" in Article IV. Finally, he could have added it, along with some of the other language he proposed, to the Preamble of the Constitution as part of a statement of constitutional philosophy.

A final conservative interpretation comes closer to the mark. The "conservative" view that comes closest to getting the right answer is the libertarian one. (The reason for the quotation marks is that the relationship between libertarians and mainstream conservatives is as much a marriage of convenience as a true meeting of minds.) Unlike movement conservatives, who believe in the vigorous application of government authority as long as it does not impair their own interests, libertarians genuinely believe in small government. The problem is that they cannot distinguish between corporate business interests and individual liberty. Still, unlike many conservatives, libertarians are willing to take the Ninth Amendment seriously.

The libertarian view espoused by writers like Randy Barnett is that the Ninth Amendment creates a general presumption in favor of liberty, rather than requiring the identification of specific protected rights. In pursuing this analysis, Barnett has done important work in sifting the historical record. His analysis is partly right, where all the other conservative analyses are wrong, in stressing the connection between the Ninth Amendment and individual rights. But his analysis then makes the mistake of confusing rights, which come in discrete packages, and liberty, which is a vaguer concept of unrestricted action. The Amendment clearly speaks in terms of *rights* rather than some undifferentiated concept of liberty.

Thus, in the end, the full-blown libertarian interpretation is a poor fit for the language of the Ninth. It is also implausible in terms of Madison's intentions. It seems unlikely that Madison was trying to handcuff the federal government by imposing severe general limits on its powers. It bears remembering that the Ninth Amendment was the product of Madison's mind. At that point, Madison was still the pro–federal government author of the Federalist Papers, not the advocate of limited government and states' rights that he later became in reaction to Hamilton's programs. Of course, by protecting individual rights against the federal government, the Amendment in effect limited federal power and provided more breathing room for the states, but these were not the primary goals.

The language of the Ninth Amendment is not particularly obscure. It says that some of the rights retained by the people are listed in the Constitution and others are not, and the existence of the list does not carry any negative implication about the unlisted ones. Most of the listed rights in the Bill of Rights, like religious freedom and procedural rights for criminal defendants, provide guarantees against specific abuses of individuals; presumably, the unlisted rights alluded to in the Ninth are generally of the same character.

Glossary of Legal Terminology

Bill of Attainder: A legislative act finding an individual or group of individuals guilty of a crime rather than providing the right to a trial. One of the few individual rights provisions of the 1789 Constitution is a prohibition on bills of attainder. A related prohibition concerns ex post facto laws, which are laws retroactively making an act criminal or increasing the penalty.

Bill of Rights: The first ten amendments of the Constitution (or sometimes used to refer to only the first eight). The Bill of Rights devotes most of its attention to the rights of criminal defendants, providing a right to counsel, a ban on self-incrimination, protections against unreasonable searches, the right to cross-examine witnesses, etc. The First Amendment protects freedom of speech and religion.

Burger Court: The Supreme Court under the leadership of Chief Justice Warren Burger (basically the 1970s through the mid-1980s). The Burger Court was expected to lead a constitutional counterrevolution against the Warren Court but contented itself with nibbling away at Warren Court doctrines.

Civil law: The system of law used on the European continent (particularly by France and Germany) but copied elsewhere in the world. Based on comprehensive legislative codes rather than court decisions.

Common law: A body of law developed by the courts rather than by the passage of statutes by the legislature and originally created by the English courts based on a mixture of their own past decisions, community customs, the law of nations, and their sense of justice. Today, it refers to judge-made law on subjects such as contract enforcement or property rights. The first year of law school is mostly dedicated to studying the common law.

Countermajoritarian difficulty: Refers to the fact that when the Supreme Court invalidates a law, it is acting as an unelected group of judges to overturn the decision of a majority of some legislature or electorate. This is a "difficulty" because of its arguably antidemocratic character.

Dred Scott: An infamous Supreme Court decision before the Civil War. The majority held that blacks could never become citizens of the United States and that Congress lacked the power to ban slavery in the western territories. The first of these holdings was reversed by the first sentence of the Fourteenth Amendment, which makes anyone born or naturalized within the United States a citizen. The second holding was overturned by the Thirteenth Amendment.

Enumerated rights: Rights specifically listed in the Constitution, such as free speech (First Amendment) and the right to remain silent (Fifth Amendment).

Federalism: The allocation of power between the national government and state governments.

Federalists: A confusing term that was used before the Constitution went into effect to include its supporters, but afterward to include only a faction headed by Alexander Hamilton that favored strong government.

Federalist Papers: Key writings arguing in favor of the ratification of the Constitution, almost all of which were written by James Madison and Alexander Hamilton.

First Congress: The first elected senators and representatives after the Constitution went into effect. This term is confusing because there actually were earlier sessions of Congress (for example, the Continental Congress during the Revolutionary War). Many key statutes date from the First Congress. Its views about constitutional issues are also often given special weight because it included so many of the Framers of the Constitution such as James Madison.

Fugitive Slave Clause: A provision of the 1789 Constitution that required runaway slaves to be returned to their masters, even if they had escaped to a free state. It is one reason why some abolitionists considered the Constitution a pact with the devil. (Congress also passed a statute, the Fugitive Slave Act, to enforce the clause.)

Fundamental rights: Rights whose infringement requires some stronger justification than the rational basis test provides. That is, there must be at least a reasonable explanation for the government's infringement of the right, if not a compelling one. Usually the term is used with reference to unenumerated rights.

Habeas corpus: A writ issued by a court to review the legality of detention. For instance, the Supreme Court ruled that the federal courts had jurisdiction to issue habeas corpus writs on behalf of suspected terrorists detained at Guantanamo Bay.

Incorporation Doctrine: The theory that the Due Process Clause of the Fourteenth Amendment "incorporates" the Bill of Rights, so that enumerated rights such as freedom of speech and the ban on cruel and unusual punishment apply to the federal government as well as the states.

International human rights: A body of individual rights recognized since World War II in a series of treaties such as U.N. conventions and in decisions by tribunals such as the European Court of Human Rights. Also used in this book to include rights recognized under other national constitutions such as the Canadian Charter or the German Basic Law.

Judicial activism: Judicial activism can mean (a) a failure to follow the original intent, (b) overruling precedents without justification, (c) using overly aggressive remedies for violations of rights, (d) reaching the merits of cases that should have been dismissed on procedural grounds, or (e) invalidating more laws than the critics find justified. Liberals view Justices Thomas and Scalia as being activists (on grounds b, d, and e), while conservatives find Justices Kennedy and Stevens to be activists (on grounds a, c, and e).

Judicial restraint: The opposite of judicial activism (whatever that means). The meaning is that judges are trying to follow the law rather than cook up legal rationalizations for implementing their political views.

Judicial review: The power of a court to invalidate an action by the legislature or executive branch. In discussions of constitutional law, the term usually refers specifically to the power of the courts to declare legislation unconstitutional. This was established in an early Supreme Court decision called *Marbury v. Madison.* Today, judicial review is a feature of constitutions in many countries such as Canada, India, Israel, and Germany.

Jurisprudence: Used to refer either to the philosophy of law or to a specific body of law (such as "the Supreme Court's voting rights jurisprudence").

Law of nations: A body of law, recognized by the Framers of the 1789 Constitution, the Bill of Rights, and the Fourteenth Amendment, which derived from a combination of common law, moral philosophy, and international law.

Natural rights: Rights belonging to all human beings, whether or not recognized by the laws of the nation in which they reside. Classically, these rights were thought to derive from God or from a social contract that created society.

Originalism: The theory that the Constitution should be interpreted solely on the basis of the original understanding at the time it was adopted. Most originalists make an exception for issues that have been settled by precedent. Originalism was a reaction to the theory of the "living Constitution." (Under that theory, the meaning of the Constitution evolves over time in response to changing values and social needs.) On the current Supreme Court, Justices Scalia and Thomas are the most important advocates of originalism. Originalists vary in terms of the relative importance they attach to the intentions of the drafters of a constitutional provision, the understanding of the ratifiers of the provision, or the general usage of terms during the period in question.

Procedural due process: The right to a fair hearing, whether in a criminal case or a civil case (usually a suit for damages) or sometimes in a proceeding before an administrative agency.

Ratification: The approval of a constitutional provision after it is proposed, in order for it to become effective. The original Constitution provided that it would go into effect when ratified by nine states. Later amendments require ratification by three-quarters of the state legislatures, which is a considerable barrier to adoption.

Rational basis test: The minimal level of scrutiny courts use when reviewing the constitutionality of a statute. In its purest form, it requires only that the statute have some conceivable tendency, however small, to advance some legitimate governmental interest, however minor. Sometimes courts say they are applying the rational basis test but actually apply a tougher standard, requiring the justification for a law to be not only conceivable but plausible. This is often called "rational basis with teeth."

Reconstruction Amendments: Refers to the Thirteenth, Fourteenth, and Fifteenth Amendments, all of which were adopted in the period immediately after the Civil War. Southern states were not seated in Congress when some of these amendments were proposed but were required to ratify them as a precondition of readmission to the Union.

Retroactive legislation: Laws applying to conduct that took place before they were passed. The Constitution strictly limits the ability of states to pass such laws but gives the federal government broader power to do so (except in criminal statutes).

Separation of powers: The constitutional rules that apply to conflicts among the executive, legislative, and judicial branches.

Stare decisis: The principle of following precedents even when later judges might otherwise have reached a contrary conclusion.

Strict construction: An approach to constitutional interpretation stressing original intent but governed by an overall purpose of giving a restrictive reading to federal powers and to individual rights guarantees.

Social contract theory: The theory that society is based on a contract among individuals to advance their mutual interests and protect their rights. Some early versions of the theory may have assumed that such a contract was actually made as a historical event, but more often the contract is taken as a metaphor for the "consent of the governed."

State constitutional rights: Rights recognized by a state's constitution. States cannot deny the rights that the Supreme Court has recognized in the federal constitution but are free to grant additional rights in their state constitutions. Even when a state constitution uses the same language as the federal constitution (such as "due process" or "freedom of speech"), state courts can interpret that language more broadly than the federal courts. For example, as currently construed by the Supreme Court, the U.S. Constitution does not protect the right of individuals to pass out leaflets in private shopping malls. Some state constitutions have been interpreted to do so.

Statutory construction: The interpretation and application of statutes by courts. This sounds easy but often involves difficult judgment calls about how to apply language in unforeseen circumstances.

Textualism: Basically the same as originalism, but puts more stress on the commonly understood meaning of particular words and phrases.

Tort: A wrongful act that causes damage, such as assaulting another person or causing an accident through negligence.

Unenumerated rights: Rights not specifically listed in the Constitution. An example is the right to travel freely across state lines, which is not expressly protected by the Constitution.

Warren Court: Refers to the Supreme Court of the 1950s and 1960s, when Chief Justice Earl Warren was on the bench. Many of the Court's most famous decisions come from this period, such as *Brown v. Board of Education* (the desegregation decision), *Miranda* (source of the rights of the same name), *Baker v. Carr* (one person/one vote). The Warren Court is sometimes considered the epitome of judicial activism; much of the last three decades of judicial decisions can be seen as responses to the Warren Court. *Roe v. Wade* seems as if it should have been a Warren Court decision, but it was actually decided several years after Chief Justice Warren retired.

Notes

PREFACE

1. Daniel A. Farber and Suzanna Sherry, *A History of the American Constitution*, 2nd ed. (St. Paul: Thomson/West, 2005).

CHAPTER 1

1. *Griswold v. Connecticut*, 381 U.S. 479 (1965).
2. John Locke, *Two Treatises of Government*, 2nd Treatise § 135 (1690).
3. Leonard Krieger, *The Politics of Discretion: Pufendorf and the Acceptance of Natural Law* (Chicago: University of Chicago Press, 1965), 1.
4. Jack N. Rakove, *Original Meanings: Politics and Ideas in the Making of the Constitution* (New York: Alfred A. Knopf, 1996), 329.
5. *Planned Parenthood of Southeastern Pennsylvania v. Casey*, 505 U.S. 833, 851 (1992).

CHAPTER 2

1. Bernard Bailyn, *To Begin the World Anew: The Genius and Ambiguities of the American Founders* (New York: Alfred A. Knopf, 2003), 4–5.
2. Jack N. Rakove, *Original Meanings: Politics and Ideas in the Making of the Constitution* (New York: Alfred A. Knopf, 1996), 290n.
3. For an extensive discussion of Coke's dictum and its extraordinary influence in America, see Calvan Massey, *Silent Rights: The Ninth Amendment and the Constitution's Unenumerated Rights* (Philadelphia: Temple University Press, 1995), 27–30.
4. R. H. Helmholz, "Natural Law and Human Rights in English Law: From Bracton to Blackstone," *Ave Maria Law Review* 3 (2005): 1–22.

5. Ibid., 21.

6. Rakove, *Original Meanings*, 293n.

7. James Kent, *Commentaries on American Law*, 4 vols., ed. Oliver Wendell Holmes Jr. (Boston: Little, Brown, 1896), 1:2.

8. Ibid., 1:3.

9. 41 U.S. (16 Pet.) 1 (1842).

10. *Sosa v. Alvarez-Machain*, 542 U.S. 692, 731 (2004).

11. *Murray* v. The Schooner Charming Betsy, 6 U.S. (2 Cranch) 64, 118 (1894).

12. *The Nereide*, 13 U.S. (9 Cranch) 388, 423 (1815).

13. Harold Koh, "International Law as Part of Our Law," *American Journal of International Law* 98 (2004): 44.

14. Ibid., 57.

CHAPTER 3

1. Daniel A. Farber and Suzanna Sherry, *A History of the American Constitution*, 2nd ed. (St. Paul: Thomson/West, 2005), 318–19n.

2. Jonathan Elliot, ed., *Elliot's Debates: The Debates in the Several State Conventions on the Adoption of the Federal Constitution as Recommended by the General Convention at Philadelphia in 1787*, 2nd ed. (Philadelphia: Lippincott, 1937 [1836–45]), 2:454.

3. Ibid.

4. James Wilson, speech in Pennsylvania, November 28, 1787, in Merrill Jensen, ed., *Documentary History of the Ratification of the Constitution* (Madison: State Historical Society of Wisconsin, 1976), 2:388.

5. Elliot, ed., *Elliot's Debates*, 4:316 (January 18, 1788).

6. Jack N. Rakove, *Original Meanings: Politics and Ideas in the Making of the Constitution* (New York: Alfred A. Knopf, 1996), 330n.

7. Ibid., 310n.

8. *Annals of Congress*, 1st Cong., 759.

9. Ibid., 759–60.

10. Ibid., 760.

11. Rakove, *Original Meanings*, 329n.

12. Joseph Story, *Commentaries on the Constitution*, 5th ed. (Boston: Little, Brown, 1905 [1891]), 1:651.

CHAPTER 4

1. Randy E. Barnett, ed., *The Rights Retained by the People: The History and Meaning of the Ninth Amendment* (Fairfax, Va.: George Mason University Press, 1989), 1:64.

CHAPTER 5

1. 3 U.S. (3 Dall.) 386 (1798)

2. 10 U.S. (6 Cranch) 87 (1810),

3. For further discussion, see G. Edward White, *The American Judicial Tradition: Profiles of Leading American Judges* (New York: Oxford University Press, 1976), 14–17; William E. Nelson, "The Eighteenth-Century Background of John Marshall's Constitutional Jurisprudence," *Michigan Law Review* 76 (1978): 893, 932, 936.

4. William H. Pease and Jane H. Pease, eds. *The Antislavery Argument* (Indianapolis: Bobbs-Merrill, 1965), 391–92. Chase was "astonished" at the view that a majority could rightfully enslave a minority. See Eric Foner, *Free Soil, Free Labor, Free Men: The Ideology of the Republican Party Before the Civil War* (New York: Oxford University Press, 1970), 132. For more on Chase's views, see Albert Bushnell Hart, *Salmon Portland Chase*, American Statesmen 28 (Boston: Houghton, Mifflin, 1899), 67–81, 127–28.

CHAPTER 6

1. *Congressional Globe*, 31st Cong., 1st Sess., App. 265 (1850).

2. *Congressional Globe*, 31st Cong., 1st Sess., App. 1023 (1850). See generally Glyndon G. Van Deusen, *William Henry Seward* (New York: Oxford University Press, 1967), 584n14.

3. *Congressional Globe*, 36th Cong., 2nd Sess., App. 83 (1861) (emphasis in original).

4. Russell B. Nye, *Fettered Freedom: Civil Liberties and the Slavery Controversy, 1830–1860* (rev. ed.; East Lansing: Michigan State University Press, 1963), 269.

5. *Congressional Globe*, 35th Cong., 1st Sess., App. 543 (1858) (emphasis in original).

6. *Congressional Globe*, 34th Cong., 1st Sess., App. 749 (1856). Wade particularly relied on Thomas Jefferson for support.

7. *Congressional Globe*, 31st Cong., 1st Sess., App. 264 (1850).

8. *The Political Debates Between Abraham Lincoln and Stephen A. Douglas in the Senatorial Campaign of 1858 in Illinois* (New York: G. P. Putnam's Sons, 1912), 175.

9. Ibid., 64.

CHAPTER 7

1. *Congressional Globe*, 38th Cong., 1st Sess. 1424 (1864). Other references to the Declaration can be found in Sen. Henderson's remarks (1461); in Sen. Sumner's remarks (1482–83); and in Rep. Orth's remarks (*Congressional Globe*, 38th Cong., 2nd Sess. 142 [1865]). In the 1864 enabling acts for Colorado, Nevada, and Nebraska, Congress required them to follow the Declaration of Independence.

2. *Congressional Globe*, 38th Cong., 1st Sess. 1313 (1864).

3. Ibid., 2990.

4. *Congressional Globe*, 38th Cong., 2nd Sess. 138 (1865). For other general references to natural law, see 142–43 (remarks of Rep. Orth), 154–55 (remarks of Rep. Davis).

5. *Corfield v. Coryell*, 6 Fed. Cas, 546 (C.C.E.D. Pa. 1823).

6. *Congressional Globe*, 39th Cong., 1st Sess. 600 (1866). See also 476 (bill protects "fundamental rights belonging to every man as a free man"). Trumbull used somewhat similar language in connection with the Freedmen's Bureau bill (319, 322).

7. Ibid., 1118.

8. Ibid., 1835.

9. Ibid., 1757.

10. See Benjamin B. Kendrick, *The Journal of the Joint Committee of Fifteen on Reconstruction, 39th Congress, 1865–1867* (New York: n.p., 1914), 83–84; Charles Fairman, *Reconstruction and Reunion 1864–88* (New York: Macmillan, 1971), Vol. 1: 1282.

11. William E. Nelson, *The Fourteenth Amendment: From Political Principle to Judicial Doctrine* (Cambridge, Mass.: Harvard University Press, 1988). Another good overview of the Amendment is Michael Kent Curtis, *No State Shall Abridge: The Fourteenth Amendment and the Bill of Rights* (Durham, N.C.: Duke University Press, 1986).

12. John Hart Ely, *Democracy and Distrust: A Theory of Judicial Review* (Cambridge, Mass.: Harvard University Press, 1980), 28.

CHAPTER 8

1. 83 U.S. 36 (1873).

2. 198 U.S. 45 (1905).

3. *Meyer v. Nebraska*, 262 U.S. 390 (1923).

4. 526 U.S. 489 (1999).

CHAPTER 9

1. *Skinner v. Oklahoma ex rel. Williamson*, 316 U.S. 535 (1942).

2. *Moore v. City of East Cleveland*, 431 U.S. 494 (1977).

3. *Troxel v. Granville*, 530 U.S. 57 (2000).

CHAPTER 11

1. See Rebecca E. Zietlow, "Congressional Enforcement of Civil Rights and John Bingham's Theory of Citizenship," *Akron Law Review* 36, no. 4 (2003): 717–69.

2. *Washington v. Glucksberg*, 521 U.S. 702 (1997).

CHAPTER 12

1. 410 U.S. at 152.

2. Ibid., 152–53.

3. Ibid., 153. In this respect, Justice Stewart's concurring opinion was much more satisfactory (167–70, Stewart, J., concurring).

4. See Bob Woodward, "The Abortion Papers," *Washington Post*, January 22, 1989.

5. See Daniel Farber and John Nowak, "Beyond the Roe Debate: Judicial Experience with the 1980's 'Reasonableness' Test," *Virginia Law Review* 76, no. 3 (1990): 519–38.

6. See *Planned Parenthood of Southeastern Pennsylvania v. Casey*, 505 U.S. 833 (1992) (replacing the trimester system with an "undue burden" test).

7. *Morgantaler v. The Queen* [1988] 1 S.C.R. 30.

CHAPTER 13

1. 801 P.2d 617 (1990).

2. *Cruzan v. Director*, 497 U.S. 261 (1990).

3. *Washington v. Glucksberg*, 521 U.S. 702 (1997).

CHAPTER 14

1. 478 U.S. 186 (1986).

2. William N. Eskridge Jr., *Gaylaw: Challenging the Apartheid of the Closet* (Cambridge, Mass.: Harvard University Press, 1999), p. 160.

3. *Commonwealth v. Wasson*, 847 S.W.2d 487 (Ky. 1992).

4. 517 U.S. 620 (1996).

5. *Lawrence v. Texas*, 539 U.S. 558 (2003).

6. *Dudgeon v. United Kingdom*, 45 Eur. Ct. H.R. (ser. A), 4 E.H.R.R. 149 (1981).

7. 852 P.2d 44 (1993).

8. 388 U.S. 1 (1967).

9. See R. H. Helmholz, "Natural Human Rights: The Perspective of the *Ius Commune*," *Catholic University Law Review* 52 (2003): 301–25.

10. *Zablocki v. Redhail*, 434 U.S. 374 (1978).

11. 744 A.2d 864 (Vt. 1999).

12. *Goodridge v. Department of Public Health*, 798 N.E.2d 941 (2003).

13. While this book was in production, the New Jersey Supreme Court re-jected the fundamental rights argument in *Lewis v. Harris* but held that same-sex couples must be given the legal incidents of marriage, based on the view that the state constitution bars discrimination on the basis of sexual orientation.

CHAPTER 15

1. *San Antonio Independent School District v. Rodriguez*, 411 U.S. 1 (1973).

2. *Plyler v. Doe*, 457 U.S. 202 (1982).

3. *Brigham v. State of Vermont*, 692 A.2d 384 (1997).

4. *Rose v. Council for Better Education*, 790 S.W.2d 186 (Ky. 1989).

5. *Leandro v. State of North Carolina*, 488 S.E.2d 249 (1997).

6. *Hoke County Board of Education v. State*, 599 S.E.2d 365 (N.C. 2004).

7. Goodwin Liu, "Education, Equality, and National Citizenship," *Yale Law Journal* 116 (2007): 330–411.

8. 347 U.S. 483 (1954).

9. *Case Relating to Certain Aspects of the Laws on the Use of Languages in Education in Belgium*, 6 Eur. Ct. H.R. (ser. A), 1 E.H.R.R. 252 (1968).

10. Cass R. Sunstein, *The Second Bill of Rights: FDR's Unfinished Revolution and Why We Need It More than Ever* (New York: Basic Books, 2004), 145.

11. See Paul A. Minorini and Stephen D. Sugarman, "School Finance Litigation in the Name of Educational Equity: Its Evolution, Impact, and Future," in *Equity and Adequacy in Education Finance: Issues and Perspectives*, ed. Helen F. Ladd, Rosemary Chalk, and Janet S. Hansen (Washington, D.C.: National Academy Press, 1999), 49.

12. *Edgewood Independent School Dist. v. Meno*, 917 S.W.2d 717 (TX 1995).

CHAPTER 16

1. *DeShaney v. Winnebago County Dept. of Social Services*, 489 U.S. 189 (1989).

2. James Keat, *Commentaries on American Law* (1826), vol. 2, lecture 24, 15.

3. *Congressional Globe*, 39th Cong., 2nd Sess. 101 (1867) (remarks of Rep. Farnsworth). Much of this history is collected in Steven J. Heyman, "The First Duty of Government: Protection, Liberty, and the Fourteenth Amendment," *Duke Law Journal* 41, no. 3 (1991): 507–71.

CHAPTER 17

1. *Shapiro v. Thompson*, 394 U.S. 618 (1969).

2. *Haig v. Agee*, 453 U.S. 280 (1981).

3. Much of the history in this paragraph and the next comes from Zechariah Chafee, *Three Human Rights in the Constitution of 1787* (Lawrence: University Press of Kansas, 1956). Chafee wrote at the height of Cold War restrictions on travel by suspected subversives.

4. *Kelo v. City of New London*, 125 S. Ct. 2655 (2005).

5. These developments in South African law are discussed in Gregory S. Alexander, *The Global Debate Over Constitutional Property: Lessons for American Takings Jurisprudence* (Chicago: University of Chicago Press, 2006).

6. *Whalen v. Roe*, 429 U.S. 589 (1977).

7. Stephen Breyer, *Active Liberty: Interpreting Our Democratic Constitution* (New York: Alfred A. Knopf, 2005), 72–73.

CHAPTER 18

1. *Washington v. Glucksberg*, 521 U.S. 702 (1997).

CHAPTER 19

1. William Rehnquist, "Constitutional Courts—Comparative Remarks," in *Germany and Its Basic Law: Past, Present, and Future: A German-American Symposium*, ed. Paul Kirchhof and Donald P. Kommers, Dräger Foundation Series 14 (Baden-Baden: Nomos, 1993), 412.

2. *Roper v. Simmons*, 125 S. Ct. 1200 (2005).

3. *United States v. Then*, 56 F.3d 464, 469 (2nd Cir. 1995).

4. *Foster v. Florida*, 537 U.S. 990, 990* (2002).

5. Jeremy Waldron, "Foreign Law and the Modern *Ius Gentium*," *Harvard Law Review* 119 (2005): 129.

6. David P. Currie, "Lochner Abroad: Substantive Due Process and Equal Protection in the Federal Republic of Germany," *1989 Supreme Court Review* (1990): 333.

7. Steven G. Calabresi and Stephanie Dotson Zimdahl, "The Supreme Court and Foreign Sources of Law: Two Hundred Years of Practice and the Juvenile Death Penalty Decision," *William and Mary Law Review* 47 (2005): 743.

8. 12 U.S. (8 Cranch) 110 (1814).

APPENDIX

1. Calvin R. Massey, *Silent Rights: The Ninth Amendment and the Constitution's Unenumerated Rights* (Philadelphia: Temple University Press, 1995), 86n.

Index